PUB WAL

IN

Buckinghamshire

Other areas covered in the Pub Walks series include:

Berkshire
Bristol and Bath
Cheshire
The Chilterns
The Cotswolds
Dartmoor and South Devon
Derbyshire
Essex
Herefordshire
Hertfordshire
The Isle of Wight
Lancashire
Leicestershire and Rutland
Lincolnshire
Middlesex and West London
Norfolk
Northamptonshire
Nottinghamshire
North Wales
Oxfordshire
Shropshire
South Wales
Surrey
The Surrey Hills
Suffolk
The Thames Valley
Warwickshire
Wiltshire
Worcestershire
East Yorkshire
North Yorkshire
South Yorkshire
West Yorkshire

A complete catalogue is available from the publisher at 3 Catherine Road, Newbury, Berkshire.

PUB WALKS IN Buckinghamshire

THIRTY CIRCULAR WALKS
AROUND BUCKINGHAMSHIRE INNS

Liz Roberts

COUNTRYSIDE BOOKS
NEWBURY, BERKSHIRE

First Published 1994

COUNTRYSIDE BOOKS
3 Catherine Road
Newbury, Berkshire

ISBN 1 85306 276 6

Designed by Mon Mohan
Cover illustration by Colin Doggett
Photographs by the author
Sketch maps by Bernard Roberts

Produced through MRM Associates Ltd., Reading
Typeset by Paragon Typesetters, Queensferry, Clwyd
Printed in England

Contents

Publisher's Note

We hope that you obtain considerable enjoyment from this book; great care has been taken in its preparation. However, changes of landlord and actual closures are sadly not uncommon. Likewise, although at the time of publication all routes followed public rights of way or well-established permitted paths, diversion orders can be made and permissions withdrawn.

We cannot accept responsibility for any inaccuracies, but we are anxious that all details covering both pubs and walks are kept up to date, and would therefore welcome information from readers which would be relevant to future editions.

Area map showing locations of the walks.

Introduction

The very 'English-ness' of the Buckinghamshire countryside endears it to the rambler: its constantly changing scenery from gentle farmland and quiet riverside meadows to chalky hills and thick beech woods. Each area has its own moods and seasonal beauty.

Through the gentle beechwood slopes of the southern Chilterns run three small rivers – the Wye, the Chess and the Misbourne – carving their way southward to join the Thames, the county's southern boundary. The beechwoods end abruptly on the crest of the steep north-facing chalk slopes of the Chilterns. The scarp slopes drop away dramatically to the rich pastureland of the northern vale, broken by ranges of low hills and fed by numerous streams. Across the hilltop strides the ancient Ridgeway track or Upper Icknield Way. The Lower Icknield Way winds along the valleys at the foot of the hills.

These 30 walks have been chosen, as far as possible, to offer at least three of the prerequisites for a satisfying walk in the Bucks countryside: some special something on which to rest the eye and recall to memory peacefulness and quiet, a variety of scenery incorporating a certain amount, though not too much, of exertion and effort and a friendly welcome in a typical village pub. I am not in a position to assure either good company or good weather!

Most of the pubs have reasonable car parks but, in the few cases where this is not so, alternative parking has been suggested. If the car is to be left in the pub car park for the duration of the walk, either before or after partaking of the pub's hospitality, it is a courtesy to ask permission of the landlord beforehand; a lone car sitting in a large pub car park after closing time *can* arouse all sorts of suspicions. Some publicans are content for customers to buy drinks and consume their own sandwiches out in the garden but equally, it is courteous to enquire before unfastening the rucksack and risking a confrontation. Opening hours have been listed and requests for muddy boots to be removed before entry noted; this latter should be as automatic to the well-mannered walker as is the 'wash-and-brush-up' before ordering your drink or food. Both dogs and children are usually welcome nowadays but both should, preferably, be well-behaved and under control. While writing this book, I have sought to ensure that the information about the pubs in it is correct; current circumstances may have since altered the way the house operates, or what it sells or cooks. I hope this will not be found by clients to be to its detriment!

The sketch map that accompanies each walk is designed to guide walkers from the starting point and give a simple and accurate idea of the route to be taken. The walks are all along public or permissive footpaths but do bear in mind that diversion orders may be made from time to time. The relevant Ordnance Survey Pathfinder map sheet is quoted for those wishing for more detail. Please observe the Country Code and close gates and leave animals undisturbed.

No special equipment is needed to enjoy the countryside on foot, but wear a stout pair of shoes and remember that there will be at least one muddy patch even on the sunniest day! I wish you many happy hours of walking in Bucks.

Liz Roberts
spring 1994

1 Chicheley
The Chester Arms

The tiny village of Chicheley, its hall and church, its pub and a group of charming cottages lie between Newport Pagnell and Bedford in the far north of the county. The countryside is gently rolling and peaceful, woodlands are small and mixed, unlike the large areas of beech woods further south and there is an air of openness and width to the horizon.

The church of St Lawrence, built in the 15th and 16th centuries, is on the approach to Chicheley Hall, a large mansion of red brick built for Sir John Chester in 1719 by Francis Smith of Warwick. The tiny lane on which both stand is opposite The Chester Arms. The Hall was the home of the Chester family for two centuries. It is now open to the public during summer weekends and bank holidays.

The Chester Arms is a hotch-potch of original buildings; its main part is Regency but other parts are all about 400 years old, as is the old bakehouse/brewhouse at the rear which was separated from the pub by a cottage of the same age. Now both are incorporated into the building, forming a sort of back to front E-shape. The old bakehouse is now decorated and furnished as a delightful small restaurant. A huge beam runs across the ceiling and supports, in part, a great loft used to store dry goods at one time. The walls are decorated with items of harness from carthorse days and there are brasses and some intriguing small pictures. The cottage, which was once the beer cellar and approached down steps from the bar, is now a quiet and restful overflow for the main bar providing space for bar meals and drinks and furnished with comfortably upholstered chairs and small tables. The trap through which the barrels of beer used to be rolled is now a pretty window with a deep sill holding china ornaments. The main bar is low-ceilinged, long and narrow and partially divided into three sections. It is pleasantly carpeted and furnished and has a warm and friendly atmosphere. There is a games machine and discreet piped music. All three parts of the inn have lovely old fireplaces.

The house is owned by Greene King so the beers on hand-pump are IPA and Abbot; Guinness is also sold on draught. Wines, three white and a red, are sold by the glass and there is a good, but fairly expensive, wine list. Food is home-made, inexpensive and good. Specials appear on a board at the end of the bar and include, always, a home-made soup (specially to be recommended is the vegetable broth brimming with all sorts of vegetables in season) served with crusty bread and butter. Excellent value is the huge portion of delicious home-baked ham and eggs served with chips or a jacket potato. Bar snacks include special 'Chester Arms' ploughman's with a choice of beef, ham or a selection of cheeses, all garnished generously with salad. Good sandwiches and a cold buffet are very reasonably priced. There are also at least five fish and vegetarian dishes and the evening menu includes a number of grills. The special Sunday menu includes two roasts and appropriate veg and a separate children's menu. Children are welcome in the cellar bar and are asked to behave with consideration for others. Meals are served every day from noon to 2 pm and from 7 pm to 9 pm, but no food is served on Sunday evenings. Outside is a very pretty and well-kept garden with plenty of picnic tables and benches. Opening hours are from 11 am to 2.30 pm and from 6 pm to 11 pm, Mondays to Fridays; on Saturdays the pub opens at 7 pm and the usual restrictions obtain on Sundays. The proximity of this pleasant and friendly pub to the M1 (junction 14) makes it a useful resting place on a journey if motorway cafeteria are not on the agenda.

Telephone: 0234 391214.

How to get there: The pub is handy for junction 14 of the M1. Follow the A509 from Newport Pagnell and, at a roundabout, take the A422 for Chicheley. The Chester Arms is on the left just into the village.

Parking: The pub has a large car park.

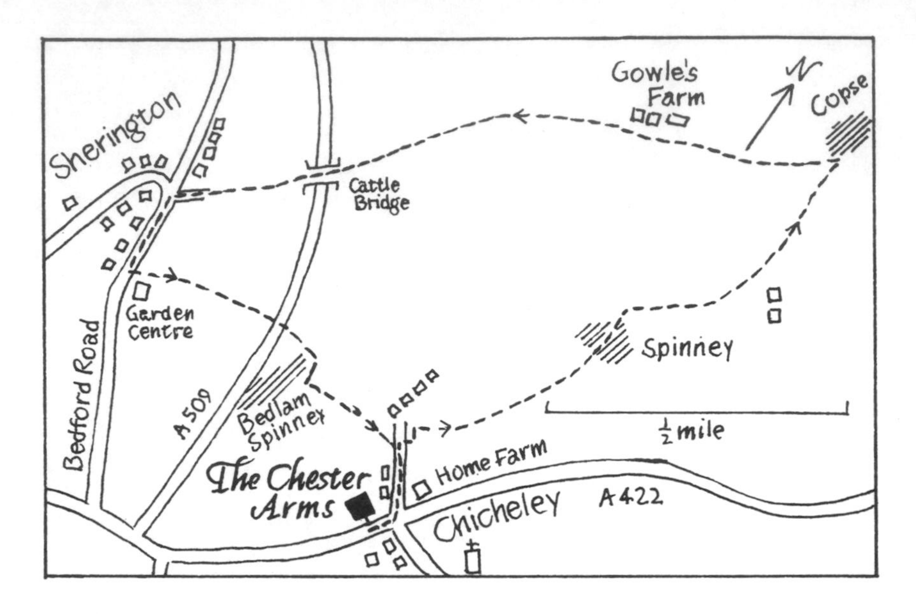

Length of the walk: 3 miles. Map: OS Pathfinder 1024 Newport Pagnell and Milton Keynes (GR 903449).

This short walk, connecting the two villages of Chicheley and Sherington, is a happy find in the north of the county, within a stone's throw of the busy, new and growing town of Milton Keynes and the hurry and bustle of the M1.

The Walk

Turn left out of the pub and left again into Bedlam Lane beside the lovely old house and barns of Home Farm and, after 400 yards or so, take the marked bridleway, turning right and then left, and follow it straight across the large field about 150 yards away from a row of houses on the left. Turn right at the field corner and follow the track, keeping the hedge on the left, to a green wooden arrow on the edge of a small spinney of poplar trees.

Here turn left and follow the path ahead through the trees to turn right on the far side and follow the field edge. After only a few yards, turn right over a stream and head straight across the next big field toward the outbuildings and yard of Grange Farm on an eminence ahead. At the top of the field turn left to follow a farm track to the right of the hedge for about ¼ mile going through marvellous, gently undulating farmland scenery. At an intersection close to a small copse turn left, almost a hairpin bend, to walk diagonally across the next field to the corner of a hedge. Here turn right and follow the path alongside the hedge and, at a gap in the hedge at the bottom of the field, walk through and across the next field to a waymark visible in the hedge on the opposite side.

Follow the path now keeping the hedge on the right. Just round the field corner go through a gap in the hedge which is waymarked and leads, over a small stream and plank bridge, straight ahead on a well-defined path with Gowle's Farm ahead on the right. Go past the farm and follow the track ahead with splendid views all around. The tower of Chicheley church stands out from among the trees on the left while, below on the right, the taller tower of Sherington church lies among the village houses and cottages. Go over the A509 by a bridge and come downhill into the outskirts of Sherington past small houses and gardens.

At a T-junction just before the village proper, turn left into Bedford Road and follow it to a marked bridleway on the left just beside a garden centre. Go over a stile and walk straight across the field to a stile tucked up in the right-hand corner of the hedge. Here the A509 must be negotiated without the aid of a bridge to reach the marked path on the far side. Cross with extreme care. Follow the path on the far side over a stile and round Bedlam Spinney, down the field with the hedge on the right and bear left at its end to follow the path emerging onto the top end of Bedlam Lane. Turn right to follow it back to the road with the Chester Arms on the right.

2 Akeley
The Bull and Butcher

In the Domesday Book this village is called Achlei; the name derives from Ake or Oak and Ley, a field. There is still a very large stand of mixed woodland close by with many fine oak trees in it. Akeley had a church as early as 1164 and its living was in the possession of Longeville Abbey. In the churchyard is the grave of Ann Clarke, who lived to be 104 years old, experiencing the reigns of seven monarchs, having been born in the reign of Charles II and dying in the reign of George III.

The Bull and Butcher, a freehouse, is a whitewashed building much of which dates back to the 17th century. It stands squarely on the corner of Church Square opposite a small building which was once Akeley School. At one time the inn was the property of New College, Oxford. In the old days many of the colleges were in the habit of purchasing property outside the city of Oxford to which their inmates would retire when catastrophes such as the Plague or the Black Death hit the city; the Bull and Butcher was such a retreat. The inn is only a few miles from Silverstone so is much patronised by motor-racing enthusiasts. The howl of tyres as the cars hurtle round the circuit is a common sound nearby.

The first part of the bar has a plain wood floor, primarily for farmers and walkers, I was told. The further end of the bar is carpeted for the gentry! The rough-cast walls are decorated with photos, not, surprisingly, of Silverstone and its aficionados, but of well-known local customers, and also with some well-accomplished drawings. There are red plush banquettes and tables on each side of a huge facing-both-ways fireplace where logs burn and crackle on cold winter days. The curved beams in the lower, old, part of the bar are unusual. The small dining-room off the bar is non-smoking and this is where the excellent cold table is laid. There is a wide and unusual variety of help-yourself salads which can be accompanied by cheese, honey-roast ham, cold beef, one of three or four home-made quiches or game pie supplied by the local butcher. All are served with either hot jacket potato or crusty granary bread, locally baked, and all at ridiculously low prices. Hot meals are served in the evenings only. The cold buffet operates at lunchtimes from Monday to Saturday, while evening meals are served from Tuesday to Saturday. No food is served on Sundays. Good value wines are sold by the bottle and three house wines, one red and two white, by the glass. Behind the bar is a dazzling array of malt whiskies and a farm cider. Well-kept beers on hand-pump are Marston's Pedigree, Morland Bitter and Old Speckled Hen, Fuller's London Pride and a guest ale. Children are permitted in the dining area and in the large and pleasant garden behind the inn.

Telephone: 0280 6257.

How to get there: Akeley lies on the A413, 2½ miles north of Buckingham and 8 miles from Towcester. The Bull and Butcher is in the centre of the village.

Parking: Car parking is in the square in front of the inn.

Length of the walk: 4½ to 5 miles. Map: OS Pathfinder 1046 Buckingham (GR 707377).

The walk, fairly long but very gentle, circumnavigates the splendid landscaped gardens of Stowe Park over lush farmland and gently undulating scenery. For the untirable, it is usually possible to visit and walk round the park, which is now in the hands of the National Trust.

The Walk

Turn left out of the pub and walk back the few yards to the A413 and turn left again at the corner to walk up the road for about ¼ mile to go over a stile on the right just past the exit of Leckhampstead Road on the left. Immediately turn left to walk across the field to a metal

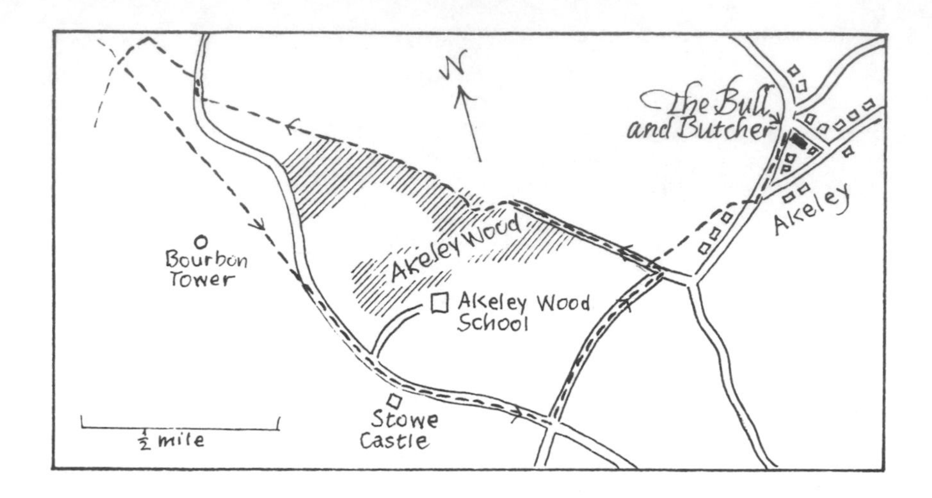

gate which has to be climbed as it is padlocked. Walk behind the gardens of a row of houses and just slightly right to a gap in the hedge by a big oak tree. Go through the gap to walk across the next small field, keeping the hedge on the right, to a stile in the hedge opposite leading on to a lane at a sharp bend. Turn right to walk up the narrow lane alongside Akeley Wood on the left. After a few yards follow the grassy track to the right of a hedge with open countryside on the right. At the end of this long field, bear left to go through the hedge on to a track where you turn right to walk on along a sometimes very muddy track through pleasant, shady mixed woodland of oak, ash and some beech.

The track emerges after about ¾ mile on to a lane with a fine view of the elegant obelisk in Stowe Park. Turn right and walk up the lane for a few yards to take the marked bridle track on the left. Here the landscape is gently undulating and parklike in aspect with small clumps of varied trees on the turf. Turn sharply left to follow the track opposite a metal gate, and after 50 yards, go over a stile on the left and across the corner of a field to another stile opposite. Now the path is absolutely dead straight ahead with a splendid view of Stowe Castle on the horizon. Go past a brake of woodland to a stile on the left on the corner of a larger area of woodland. Go over the stile. According to the map, the path leads straight ahead but it is occasionally rather difficult to follow as it is not always reinstated after ploughing and a crop of waist-high and damp broad beans can be a little daunting! The walker is legally quite entitled to walk straight ahead but may find it prudent to walk round the two sides of the field where the path finally joins a bridleway and, after a short leftward curve, a small road.

Turn right again to walk down the road past Stowe Castle on the right. This is now an elegant dwelling and behind it is the Bourbon Tower on the Stowe estate. Once a keeper's cottage, the tower was renamed to commemorate a visit of the exiled French royal family in 1808.

Soon the broad entrance to Akeley Wood School is passed on the left. There are magnificent wide views over the countryside on the right through gaps in the thick hazel hedge. Here are glimpses of Stowe Park and the village of Chackmore at its gate. At the crossroads turn left to walk back toward Akeley between wide colourful verges, rich with a great variety of tall wild flowers.

Soon the sharp bend encountered on the outward journey is reached. Go over the stile in front on the bend and across the field through the gap in the hedge and over the metal gate to the stile on to the A413 again. Turn left to walk back to the Bull and Butcher and the parked car.

Stowe gardens, created in the 18th century by Lord Cobham and Earl Temple, whose home was Stowe, are a supreme example of Georgian landscape garden design. The Elysian Fields were designed by Kent in 1730 in a naturalistic style and the buildings were designed by Kent and Vanbrugh. The house has been a public school since 1923. The grounds and park are now in the hands of the National Trust and are open to the public on most days from 10 am until dusk. Light refreshments and teas are available. You are advised to check times of opening for the house and grounds before visiting, and the telephone number is 0280 813650.

3 Great Brickhill
The Old Red Lion

Great Brickhill, where evidence of Roman and Bronze Age settlements has been found, straddles a ridge whose highest point is 500 ft above sea level. All around are panoramic views of gentle farmland and woodland and the village in its turn can be seen from many of the surrounding hamlets. Oliver Cromwell spent some time in Great Brickhill, late in the Civil War, visiting his troops who were resting while on their way from Aylesbury to Northampton. The barn in which Cromwell slept is now converted into a dwelling and is known, of course, as Cromwell Cottage. The manor of Great Brickhill has been in the ownership of the Duncombe family since the 16th century and there are still Duncombes in the village, although the original house was destroyed by fire in 1933.

The Old Red Lion lies in the centre of the village on the left-hand side of the road, opposite an attractive triangle planted with flowers and trees. Behind the pub is a small, attractive garden with a children's play area and then a lawn with picnic tables and benches. Beyond, the land falls steeply downhill affording panoramic views for miles.

Looking out over the peaceful landscape from here with not a dwelling in sight, it is difficult to believe that the huge conurbation of Milton Keynes is not much more than ten miles away.

From the garden the first, flagstoned bar in the pub is called The Den. Plainly furnished with dark wood tables and wheelback chairs, it has a fruit machine and a bar-billiards table. The deep fireplace is decorated with horse brasses as are the upright beams, and there are pleasant prints on the walls. The main bar and dining area, in which children are permitted, is large and airy and comfortably furnished; a special touch is the little vase of fresh flowers on each table. The floor is carpeted and the fireplace decorated with horse brasses. On a dark-wood dresser a variety of plates is displayed and, behind it, a grandfather clock stands importantly. Beside the door is a list of landlords dating from 1770, but, I am assured, the pub itself is much older. There are prints and photographs of the pub during various stages of its existence. The wine list is quite comprehensive and all the wines are sold by the glass or the bottle. There are three permanent real ales: Boddingtons, Brakspear and Flowers Original. The guest ale for the week when I visited was Wadworth 6X but this is often changed.

Food, home-made, is served every day between 12 noon and 2 pm and from 7 pm. Specials appear on a blackboard from time to time but there is a permanent, large menu of filling and appetising hot meals including home-made steak and mushroom pie, vegetarian lasagne and a number of fish and chicken dishes. 'Old Red Lion Specials', filled baguettes with chicken, bacon and salad, provide a filling cold meal. There are jacket potatoes with a variety of fillings and ploughman's lunches which include home-baked ham as well as a variety of cheeses and a salad garnish. The service is quick and pleasant and the loos are spotless. Opening times from Monday to Friday are from 11.30 am to 2.30 pm and 5.30 pm to 11 pm. On Saturdays the pub does not open till 6.30 pm in the evening and on Sundays the hours are from 12 noon to 3 pm and 7 pm to 10.30 pm.

Telephone: 0525 261715.

How to get there: From the A4146, Leighton Buzzard to Milton Keynes road, turn right at a crossroads just before Stoke Hammond, signposted Great Brickhill, and go over the humpy canal bridge to follow Ivy Lane into the village where the pub is on the left.

Parking: The pub's car park is fairly small but there is parking space in front and to the side.

Length of the walk: 5 miles. Map: OS Pathfinder 1071 Milton Keynes (S) and Woburn and 1047 Leighton Buzzard and Stewkley (GR 904303).

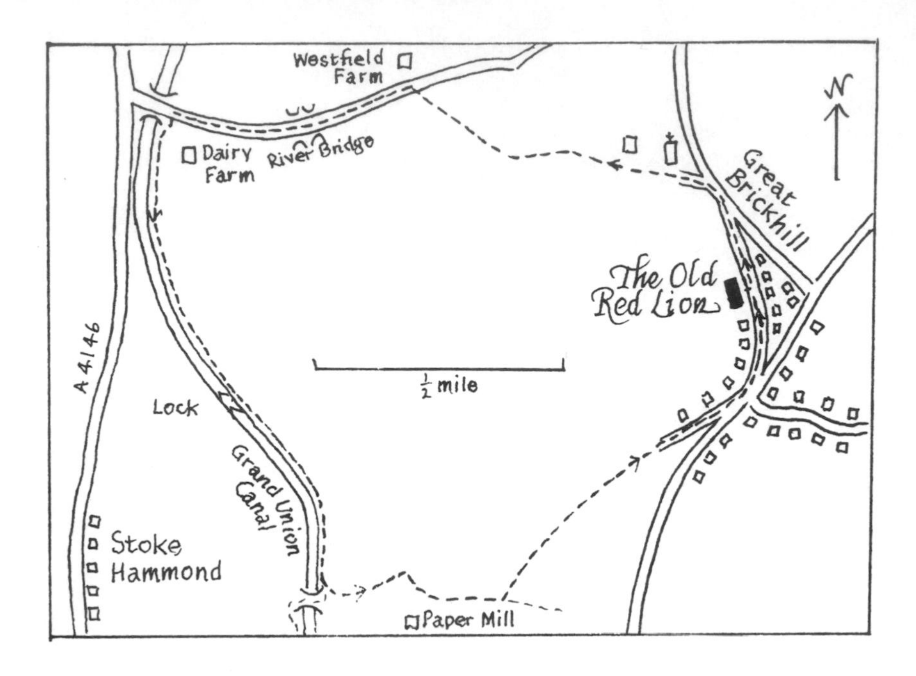

This walk is longer than some but the gradients are gentle and quite a bit of it is alongside the flower-filled banks of the Grand Union Canal on the level.

The Walk

Turn left out of the pub and walk along the pavement by the left fork in the road, past the village shop on the left and later the Duncombe Arms on the right by pretty thatched cottages and warm red-brick houses. Opposite an attractive brick house and the Castle next door to it and alongside the church of St Mary, turn left into a no through road. After 50 or so yards take a right fork on to a marked path and soon go over a stile to follow a not very distinct path alongside a high old brick wall. Behind is a splendid white house, the present home of the Duncombe family, and a view of the squat church tower behind it. There are sweet chestnut trees on the other side of the wall.

Go over another stile and keep straight on down the field and, at the turn of the wall, near the end of the field, turn right and go over a high stile to walk down and then diagonally across a field of tall grasses towards Westfield Farm. The path emerges on to a lane through a big metal gate and here turn left to follow the lane past Lower Rectory Farm where all sorts of skilful things happen like car-repairing, food-preparing, machinery-making, joinery and butchery. Go over the bridge across the river Ouzel and continue past Orchard

Mill and Old Dairy Farm on the left. At the canal bridge turn left and descend to the towpath where you keep left to follow it for about a mile. The path makes an attractive and interesting route for all who enjoy natural history, industrial archaeology and bird-watching. The canal was part of the great surge of canal building which took place, over a period of 80 years, in the late 18th and early 19th centuries to transport manufactured goods, coal, foodstuffs and farm produce about the country by means of narrowboats. In December 1793 3,000 navvies, or navigators, were employed digging out the canal which was to join up with the Regent's Canal in London and the Grand Junction Canal in Birmingham. Later on, the new Grand Union Canal Company was formed. Nowadays the canal is mainly used for leisure and the colourful boats, often with gaily filled flower boxes on their roofs, can be seen moving gently along, barely disturbing the water birds: herons, moorhens and a variety of ducks all of whom inhabit the banks of the canal.

Go under the bridge at Stoke Hammond Lock, only wide enough to hold one narrowboat at a time, and continue along the towpath with a splendid view of Great Brickhill perched above on the left. On the far side of a bridge bearing a sign to the Dolphin Inn, go by steps off the towpath and turn right to walk along a lane through white gates and soon on the right a pair of impressive wrought-iron gates and a view of the red-brick paper-mill. Shortly passing bridges over two small tributaries of the Ouzel, go on along a public bridleway to a group of farm buildings where you turn left on to an arrowed path/bridle track. Follow this, working gently uphill between high hedges with glimpses of broad arable landscape in its gaps and ignoring all cross-paths. Finally a narrow, tarmacked lane is reached; walk along this past pretty cottages on the left and, soon, the village green on the right. Bear left at the main road to return to the Old Red Lion.

4 Stewkley
The Carpenters Arms

At two miles in length, Stewkley undoubtedly has the longest village high street in England. It is divided almost equally between north and south sides by its magnificent squat Norman church. The villagers refer to the division as 'Uptown' and 'Downtown' and at one time a friendly rivalry existed between the two. Set among yew trees, the church of St Michael, with its squat, square tower and splendidly recessed west door, is the finest Norman building in the county and one of the best examples of its period in England. It was carefully and thoughtfully restored by G.E. Street in 1862, retaining the original plan and altering only the steeply pitched roof. Much of the housing in the High Street is of 19th and 20th century origin but tucked among these are charming whitewashed and thatched cottages, 17th and 18th century farmhouses and the houses of well-to-do merchants. Manor Farm is 16th century and timber-framed with fascinating diagonal chimney stacks and a dovecote reputed to contain 800 nests, while 16th century No 14 Ivy Lane was the country home of Mrs Pankhurst and her daughter Sylvia. Who can tell what plots were hatched between those walls? Stewkley, along with Wing and Cublington, had to fight for its very survival in the late 1960s when plans to build a third London airport here would have annihilated the village, church and all.

The Carpenters Arms lies at the very southernmost end of the High Street South, a pleasant square red-brick building of uncertain date but said to be around 300 years old. You would not need to be very tall to crash your head on the low-beamed ceilings of the two bars and the tiny dining-room. The public bar, with games machines, is on the left and the lounge bar on the right of the entrance with the cosy restaurant behind it. The bars are furnished in dark green upholstered banquettes and chairs and stools which surround light-wood, decoratively carved tables. The floor is mostly carpeted but the entrance is flagged. The piped music is discreet and the welcome from the landlady and her staff is warm, the service prompt and efficient. There is no garden, but children, if well behaved, are welcome in the bars and there are tables and benches outside at the front. Well-kept Bass, Tetley, John Bull and Courage Best are all on hand-pump as is Scrumpy Jack cider. There is a very good list of carefully kept wines and three house wines, two white and a red, are served by the glass. Much to be recommended is the fresh plaice and 'proper' chips at a give-away price, venison pâté and the delicious home-made soups, served with a large hunk of crusty French bread. The large menu of restaurant meals includes meat, chicken and fish dishes – 14 of them – and vegetarian meals all very reasonably priced. There is a wide range of tempting home-made sweets and a big menu of bar snacks, including chicken or scampi in a basket, ploughman's lunches, French bread served with cheese or home-roast ham and sandwiches with a choice of six fillings. Opening hours are from 11 am to 11 pm except on Sundays when the usual restrictions obtain.

Telephone: 0525 240272.

How to get there: From Aylesbury take the A418 for Leighton Buzzard and at Wing bear left off the A418 towards Soulbury. Take the next turning left on to an unclassified road to follow it for 2½ miles into Stewkley where the Carpenters Arms is on the right just into the village.

Parking: This is limited on the right of the inn but is seldom crowded.

Length of the walk: 5½ to 6 miles. Map: OS Pathfinder 1071 Leighton Buzzard and Stewkley (GR 854253).

This is a walk for the sturdy, agile and dedicated. It is quite a long one across countryside which can be muddy and most of the numerous stiles are double ones

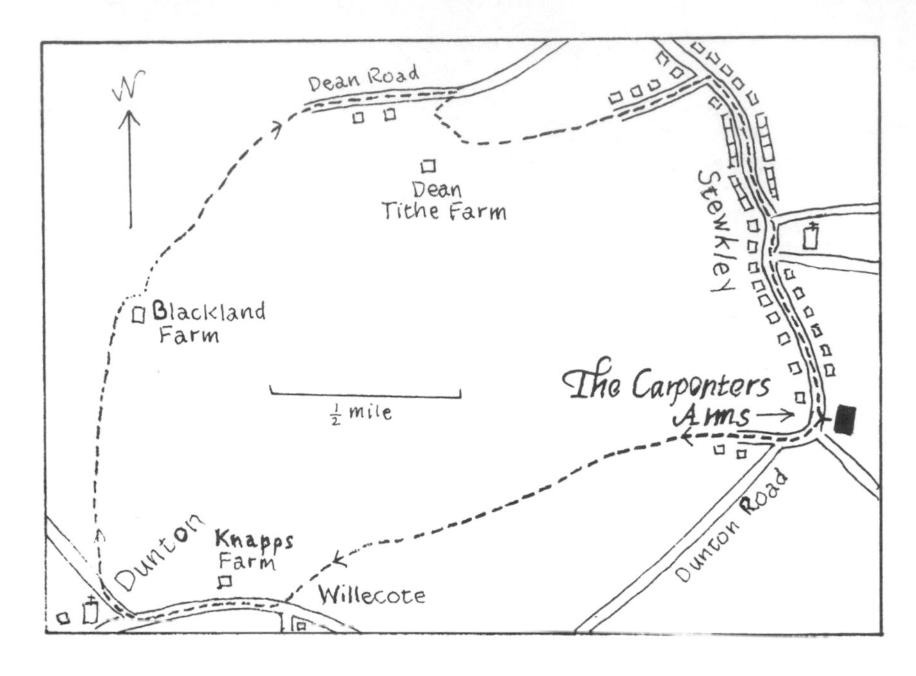

and high with it! The stupendous long views over the peaceful countryside and farmland make it well worth the effort.

The Walk

Cross the road to walk down the road opposite, Dunton Road, past pleasant old houses and cottages and soon turn right into South Lane, a narrow no through road. At the brick entrance to the house called Bracrina, bear left to follow the marked path beside a wire fence and with a view of a delightful pond. After the two disastrous droughts in the late 1970s, the National Farmers' Union recommended farmers to dig themselves 'reservoirs' so that they would have a supply of water in case of a ban. This pond looks man-made and has a charming border of water-loving plants and reeds and a beautifully peaceful look with a small population of ducks.

Follow this path ahead over fields and stiles, ignoring a stile on the left signposted Cublington. After the next stile, about 150 yards ahead, take the path on the left and then turn right to follow the path ahead again but now with the hedge on the right instead of the left. Continue across fields and over double stiles, then finally across the last small field towards the buildings of Littlecote Farm to a gate which leads on to a lane where you turn right to walk towards the tiny hamlet of Dunton past Knapps Farm. Dunton church lies just a little past the right turn in the lane which you take to walk along for about 300 yards before taking a marked path on the right over a gate opposite the entrance to Dunton Manor. Follow the path ahead, at first keeping the hedge close on the left with magnificent views to the north of Aylesbury Vale on the right. At a gate cross over, keeping the tall, thick hedge now on the right and walk straight ahead across an open field, crossing a track at the gate to follow the path through the next gate.

Walk along the wood edge on the right until a stile in the hedge is reached on the right. Go over the stile and straight ahead past the side of Blackland farmhouse and, on the far side, turn left to follow the tarmacked bridleway ahead for about ¾ of a mile. At an intersection with Dean Road bear right to walk along the narrow lane past a group of big rusty old barns. After about ¼ mile turn right on to a concrete drive toward Dean Tithe Farm and cross the stile on the left at a corner about 250 yards ahead. Now follow the path, with the church on the skyline dead ahead. Walk across the next field to a double stile in the right-hand corner and then, 20 yards on, another pair in the hedge. Follow the path along the field with the hedge on the right, over another double stile on the right and straight across the next field to a gap in the left corner.

Immediately go over the stile on the right and follow the narrow path round a rather murky little pond to a stile on the far side, then follow the obvious path diagonally over three fields (and stiles) to a bungalow on a lane.

Turn left at the bungalow to walk up past a little row of cottages on the left to the main street of Stewkley alongside the Swan. Here turn right to walk ahead down the long High Street, past the church and bearing right at a fork into High Street South towards Wing and Aylesbury. The Carpenters Arms is on the right after another ½ mile or so.

5 Quainton
The George and Dragon

The H-shaped pattern of delightful village lanes is outlined with old and mellow red-brick houses and cottages, some tiled, some thatched leading up to the green slopes of Quainton Hill, an abrupt elevation some 187 metres above sea level. The cross-bar of the H is formed by the village green, which slopes down from the convergence of Upper Street with Church Street at Cross Farm to the Strand below. At the top of the green is a stone cross which is said to be a Saxon preaching cross, erected before the 14th century church was even thought of. Cross Farm is of chequered brick with a carved stone panel dated 1723 over the nine-panelled central door. It was built by Justice Dormer of the Court of Common Pleas for one of his daughters. The Dormer family lived for many generations in the village and there is a monument in the church to Justice Dormer, who died in 1726. Behind Cross Farm is a huge windmill designed and built by a local man, James Anstiss, between 1830 and 1832. It was built without scaffolding, floor by floor, of locally made clay bricks and the sails were driven by an engine. It has not been in use since 1881. (See photograph page 29)

The George and Dragon is on the village green, next door to the butcher and almost opposite the post office. It is a very typical village pub, right on the road with only a few tables and benches outside its front door on to the green by way of a garden. Tucked in behind it are two tiny cottages with rampaging colour-filled gardens in summertime. The pub is divided into a public and a saloon bar, the saloon being the oldest (probably 17th to early 18th century) part and the public bar a later addition. The entrance is flagged but the bar floors are carpeted, the saloon pleasantly furnished with deep red plush upholstered stools and banquettes set around plain dark-wood tables. A deep arch, which at one time could have been a fireplace, separates the two sections of the bar. Children are welcome in the back part and there is a special menu for them. The public bar has a billiards table, a fruit machine and a juke box.

Three real ales are sold: Bass, Tetley and Benskins. There is an extensive wine list and five house wines are sold by the glass. Bar snacks and meals are served at lunchtimes and in the evenings every day except Sunday when no meals are served in the evening. The food is home-made and the specialities are very delicious home-made pies; chicken and fish dishes are on the menu as are steak and mixed grills, all at ridiculously low prices. Especially good value is a steak sandwich: a white roll containing two large minute steaks served with a salad. There is a choice of seven sandwich fillings and an excellent filler is a large chunk of French bread filled with bacon and then lavishly spread with cheese which is then grilled till brown and crisp. The service is efficient; the landlord and his wife are young and welcoming. Opening hours are from noon to 2.30 pm and from 6 pm to 11 pm; on Sundays from noon to 3 pm and from 7 pm to 10.30 pm.

Telephone: 0296 75436.

How to get there: Take the A412 from Aylesbury toward Bicester and at a crossroads 1 mile from Waddesdon turn right on an unclassified road signposted Oving and Quainton. After a mile turn left at a crossroads and follow the road into the village. Just past the White Hart public house turn right on to the village green and the George and Dragon is on the right just a few yards up.

Parking: There is very little traffic around the green so it is quite permissible to leave your car parked outside the pub during the walk but it is advisable to let the landlord know that it might be there for some time.

Length of the walk: 5 miles. Map: OS Pathfinder 1070 Winslow and Stratton Audley (GR 745203).

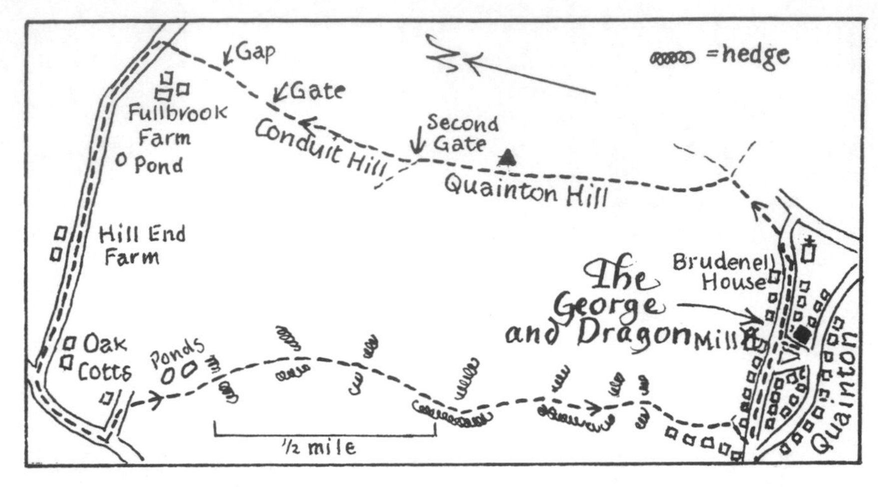

The walk climbs out of Quainton village to offer some super views of the Vale of Aylesbury all around and returns following paths across lush meadows with the hills high on the left.

The Walk

Turn right out of the pub to walk alongside the green past the butcher's shop and turn right again into Church Street to walk along it for about ¼ mile between delightful picturesque old houses and cottages and, on the right, the splendidly preserved 17th century Winwood almshouses. On the left is Brudenell House, once the rectory, an impressive 16th century house of red and grey brick. Ahead is the church of St Mary and the Holy Cross, mainly of 14th century origin. The north aisle has four late 15th century painted panels depicting saints. There are figures of Richard Brett, one of the translators of the Authorised Version of the Holy Bible, who died in 1637 and of Richard Winwood who founded the adjoining almshouses.

Follow the road downhill past the gate of Brudenell House and a splendid view of the Queen Anne frontage which replaced the original brickwork. Take the marked path on the left just beyond the gate over two stiles and fields to a marked bridleway in the right corner of the second field. Here turn left on to the bridleway and through a wooden gate to climb steadily up Quainton Hill along the well-defined track towards a TV mast on the summit. Look back, at the halfway stage, on the panoramic view of the whole Vale of Aylesbury laid out below, Quainton windmill in the foreground and, high up, silhouetted against the skyline, Waddesdon Manor amongst dark trees just to the left of the mill. From the summit it is possible to see the whole of North

The Cross Farm Windmill

Bucks, Didcot Power Station's cooling towers in Oxfordshire and, it is reputed, the hills of Shropshire.

From the summit follow the track ahead past the mast and a small reservoir with the tall chimneys of London Brickworks at Calvert on the left and huge, uncluttered and peaceful views of farmland all around with the red roofs of the houses in the village of North Marston away on the right.

Turn right at the second gate after the mast to walk gently down Conduit Hill toward Fulbrook Farm below. The track leads into a pronounced dip with the farm buildings well to the left. Go through the small gate at the foot of the hill and across the next field, through an obvious gap in the hedge opposite, and across the field ahead to a rusty metal gate leading on to the farm track. Here turn right and then left on reaching the lane ahead where soon there is a beautiful willow tree overhanging a rushy pond with hills rising steeply beyond.

Walk on down the lane for about a mile past Hill End Farm and Oak Cottages, ignoring all the tempting footpath turnings, till the main road is reached. Here turn left and walk along this quite busy road for 400 yards or so to take a farm track on the left opposite a footpath sign on the right. After 100 yards go over the stile on the right to follow the footpath round the side of two medieval fish ponds on the left to a pair of stiles in the hedge opposite. Go over the stiles and cross the field bearing half-right to a stile in the far right corner and, over it, turn right to follow the path alongside the thickset hedge to a stile tucked right up in the far corner on the right. Follow the path straight ahead with the TV mast just visible high up on the left. Continue over the next stile to a metal gate on the far side of the next field. Go over this gate and then immediately through a gate on the left to follow the path across fields and over stiles to a narrow hedged grassy track. Follow this to a T-junction where you turn right. At the road turn left and then left again at its junction to follow Upper Street back to the village green and the George and Dragon now downhill on the left.

6 Whitchurch
The White Swan

Whitchurch enjoys a commanding position on a low ridge of hills with fine views to the south-west over the Vale of Aylesbury. The older part is at the top of the High Street where earthworks of the once important Bolebec Castle, destroyed by Roundhead forces during the Civil War, can be seen. Rex Whistler stood on the mount to paint his best-known *View of the Vale*. Below it there is a fascinating mix of 17th and 18th century houses and cottages and some more modern interlopers. The church of St John is of pale, almost white, limestone giving the village its name, White-church. The White Swan is at the newer, Aylesbury, end of the High Street and stands a little back from the road. Much of it is of warm old red brick and tile but a small part is still thatched. Outside on the front wall is an ancient pump. Behind the inn there is an enormous lawned garden with plentiful picnic tables and benches under trees. Inside the odd-shaped saloon bar a warm welcome awaits the visitor from the cheerful landlord and his wife who serve this bar and another, smaller, Sam's bar, from a very small counter. Service is miraculously fast as a trio of young women hurry to and fro balancing plates of food as if born to it or helping at the bar itself. The inn fills up quickly as it is a popular local rendezvous

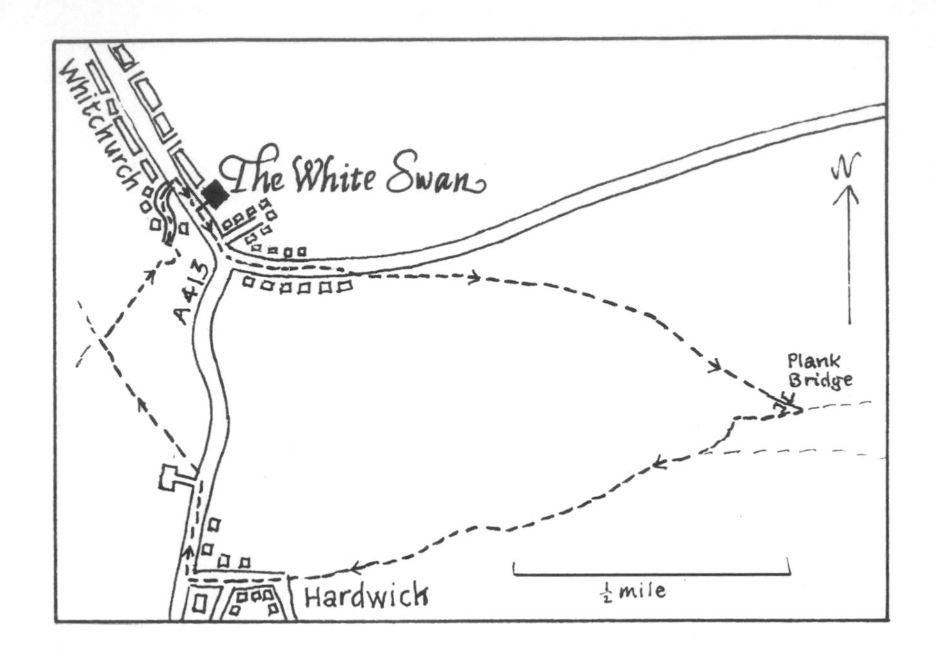

and a pleasant place at which to break a journey. The low-beamed carpeted bar has restful warm-coloured oak panelling into which are set wooden seats. Large elderly leather armchairs and a carved Gothic-style settle surround sturdy tables and circle a brick fireplace. Oil paintings hang on the walls and the shelf above the panelling has some attractive china pieces. In the corner stands a large grandfather clock and, by the fire, a huge copper jug full of fresh flowers.

The inn has recently been sold to Fuller's so its ales on hand-pump are ESB, Chiswick and a delicious and well-kept London Pride. There is an impressive length of malt whiskies behind the bar and house wines, a red and two white, are served by the glass or bottle. The freshly cooked bar food from an extensive menu is incredibly inexpensive and delicious. As well as the usual variations on the burger/sausage theme, there are fish and vegetarian dishes and an array of omelettes. The evening menu includes more elaborate dishes and may be eaten in the charming tiny dining-room beyond the bar. Sandwiches, plain, toasted or triple-decker, and crusty French rolls have a choice of ten fillings as do the 'ploughperson's' lunches. Excellent value is a toasted sandwich enclosing a large steak, mushrooms and onions accompanied by a salad garnish. The portions are generous and the ploughperson's lunch includes an apple. There is always a home-made soup accompanied by crusty bread and butter or a roll. Children are not permitted in the bars but the restaurant is open for their use and they have the run of the garden. Opening hours are from 11 am to 3 pm and from 6 pm to 11 pm. On Sundays food is served only at midday and the usual opening restrictions obtain.

Telephone: 0296 641228.

How to get there: Whitchurch lies on the A413 Aylesbury to Buckingham road and is about 4 miles from Aylesbury town. The White Swan lies just into the village up the hill and on the right-hand side.

Parking: There is a good-sized car park on the Aylesbury side of the inn.

Length of the walk: 4 miles. Maps: OS Pathfinder 1071 Leighton Buzzard and Stewkley and 1094 Aylesbury and Tring (GR 804206).

This undemanding walk takes you through pastoral countryside with fine views of Aylesbury Vale to Hardwick village before returning via more fields and paddocks to Whitchurch.

The Walk

Turn left out of the inn and walk past the exit of Swan Close on to the road and bear left at the fork as for Cublington and Wing. Walk along the road with fine, open views away on the left. About 50 yards past the de-control sign, take the marked footpath on the right. Go over the stile and walk across the top of the field, keeping the hedge on the left. Follow the path ahead along the tops of the fields and over high double stiles with marvellous views of open countryside around Aylesbury Vale uphill and downhill. Walk past a little old red-brick barn beside the hedge and then a little downhill across a rather boggy bit of land to find the stile tucked up in the corner on the left.

Go over the stile and a narrow plank bridge across a little stream in a deep ditch and immediately turn right to walk alongside the hedges on two sides of the field, with the hedge on the right. At the end of the second side there is a wide gap in the hedge where you turn right to walk a few yards along to a broad stony track forming a T-junction. Here turn right again to follow the bold track right into the neat and pretty little village of Hardwick. Its tall grey church tower can be seen all along the track as can the cosy sight of cows grazing in small, hedged fields and in summer rolls of stacked straw baled at the field-side. The track leads over deep cattlegrids for about ½ mile.

If you want to visit the church, turn left on to the road at the end of the path; if not forge straight ahead past the old village school on the left and the chapel and the Bell Inn on the right and downhill for a few yards to the A413 where you turn right and walk along the pavement for about ¼ mile to take a marked path well concealed in the thick hedge on the left next to a building/stables called Millpeace. Go over the high stile and under a wooden bar and across the field ahead to a stile to the right of the building. Cross the next two fields by stiles, bisected by a concrete drive, and then cross three small paddocks by stiles, the last on to a small plank bridge over a ditch. Cross the next, scrubby, field to a stile opposite and turn right to follow a cross-path to a gate in the hedge. Go through this metal gate and then, almost at once, go through a small wooden gate on the left to crowd your way along a narrow path bordered, on the left, by a thick unruly hedge and, on the right, by a wire fence. Go over double stiles at the end of the path and, by stiles, across the corner of a narrow paddock to a garden path. Turn left and walk up through a white-painted wooden gate on to the drive of a house and follow it to the road. Go straight ahead on the road past pleasant houses and the exit of Firs Close to reach the main road opposite the Swan.

7 Ashendon
The Red Lion

The village of Ashendon stands isolated on a high bare hill with spectacular views outward over a deep valley and north east to Lodge Hill where Waddesdon manor peers, rather like the castle of Giant Despair, above the tree line. The Saxon church of St Mary has a stumpy little tower and is of grey stone; its interior has been over-restored but the plain late 17th century pulpit remains. There are a number of prosperous farms around the village and agriculture is its main industry. In fact, it is reported that early in the century a traveller once asked the roadman where in Ashendon a gentleman by the name of George lived. 'There b'aint no gentlemen here,' replied the roadman, 'They be all farmers!'

The Red Lion lies on the right of Lower Street, just past the church; the street ends in a strange little square surrounding a tree-filled rectangle and lanes lead off from it. The garden and large car park of the inn afford the best views of the surrounding countryside to be found. The 16th century inn is of brick and grey stone construction with a wavy tiled roof. Outside the scene is colourful with a number of hanging baskets. The inn used to be a courthouse. Inside is a large, pleasantly carpeted horseshoe-shaped bar with an assortment of differently shaped and sized tables dotted among high-backed cushioned settles and wheelback chairs. There is a huge old fireplace at the far end which burns logs voraciously in winter. On the mantlepiece is a collection of interesting old bottles and the walls are adorned with attractive and lively pictures. A hunting horn and brass stirrups decorate one wall. Children are allowed in the bar for meals and, of course, in the wide lawned garden. The whole area above the bar is massed with pump-labels of the hundreds of guest ales the inn has served from time to time. There are four permanent ales on handpump: Wadworth 6X and IPA, Adnams and Badger, and there is a weekly change of guest ales. House wines, one red and two white, are sold by the glass and there is also a good, comprehensive wine list which is not overly expensive. The mostly home-cooked food includes home-made soup, prawn platter, lasagne served with garlic bread, garlic mussels, beef and stout pie, chicken, mushroom and tarragon pie, vegetarian dishes and a selection of sweets. Large wholemeal hoagies with generous fillings of cheese, ham, bacon and sausage or prawns and served with salad provide an excellently filling snack. Opening hours are from 12 noon to 2.30 pm and 7 pm to 11 pm and on Sundays the inn closes at 10.30 pm.

Telephone: 0296 651296.

How to get there: From Aylesbury take the A418 towards Oxford and, 2 miles past Stone, take a right turn at a crossroads signposted Cuddington, Chearsley and Long Crendon. Go through Cuddington village and turn right for Ashendon, just past two small bridges over the river Thame – Cuddington Bridges. Follow the unclassified lane for 2½ miles and turn left into Lower Street by the church and the Red Lion is about 200 yards down on the right.

Parking: There is a large car park at the inn.

Length of the walk: 4½ to 5 miles. Map: OS Pathfinder 1093 Ambrosden and Waddesdon (GR 705144).

The fairy-tale castle of Waddesdon Manor dominates the skyline for much of this walk from the hill-top village of Ashendon.

The Walk

Turn left out of the pub and walk back to the church. Turn left again and, very soon, take a marked path on the right between Long Cottage and the Village Hall and follow it steeply downhill along a dip in the ground and then ahead to a stile in a wooden fence about 80 yards from the left-hand corner of the field. Go over the stile and across the

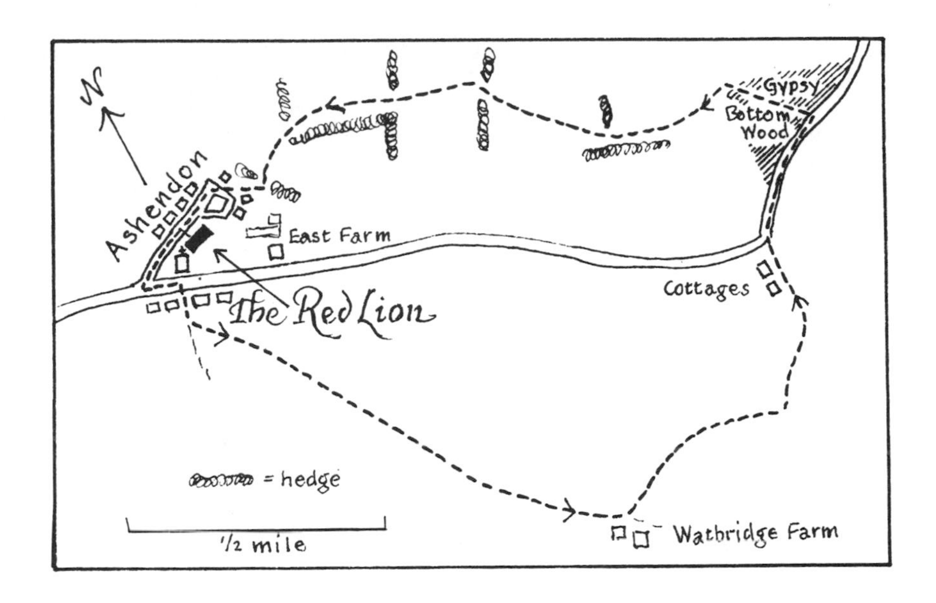

next field to a metal gate. Go through it and bear right down the field, keeping the hedge to the right, to a stile just to the left of a pond overhung with willow trees. Over the stile walk diagonally across the next field to a gate in the fence opposite. Go through the gate and follow the path diagonally across the corner of the field to two stiles set in the hedge about 75 yards from the right-hand corner of the hedge. Cross both stiles and bear left to walk across a big field making for the house and farm buildings of Watbridge Farm ahead. Waddesdon Manor stands high above the woods on the left. Go through a gate and walk to the right for a few yards to reach a farm track where you turn left to follow it past Watbridge farmhouse.

Follow the track ahead past a group of farm buildings and bear left ignoring the 'Bridleway' sign on the corner to go on up the track for about ½ mile to a trio of cottages near the main road from Ashendon to Westcott. Turn right on reaching the road to walk up for some 300 yards to take a marked footpath on the left over a small plank bridge. The footpath sign is fairly well concealed in the scrubby undergrowth. Walk ahead between wire fences through Gypsy Bottom wood. At the far end go over a stile and turn left to walk diagonally across the field to a gate in the left-hand corner by an old broken-down building where a concrete track enters from the road above. Go through the gate and straight ahead past some dilapidated buildings, possibly old ammunition dumps for the War Department depot at Westcott. Go through the next (green) metal gate and cross the next two fields by gates in the middle of the opposite hedges. Well-fed sheep and cows with their calves graze the lush valley meadows.

After the next gate walk slightly uphill across the next field keeping the hedge nearby on the left and go through another gate on the left on the far side of the field. Walk up the farm track towards the buildings of East Farm and bear right on the concrete track, circumventing a slurry pit, to arrive at a gate on the right. Go over the gate and across a small field to a stile leading into a narrow path between cottage gardens. At its end turn right on to the road past the post office and left to find the Red Lion and the parked car.

8 Marsworth
The Red Lion

The village lies at the junction of the Grand Union Canal with the Aylesbury arm, the river Ousel and the Tring reservoirs which feed the top levels of the canal. Hump-backed bridges on narrow lanes abound around the village, crossing and re-crossing the canal. The church of St Nicholas is of very early, maybe 12th century, origin and the present nave and chancel were added in the 14th century as an extension to the earlier church. There are attractive timber-framed houses and cottages in Church Lane; one in particular, Cottesloe in Vicarage Road, is a very old timber-framed house with a grotesque corbel on its roof. The reservoirs are partly in Marsworth parish and partly in Hertfordshire, which points a slim finger into Buckinghamshire at this junction. Some time ago the vicar of the parish was convinced, by the contours, that the canal had been built along the moat of an Iron Age fort close to the village and many of the villagers supported his theory by referring to the ancient Lower Icknield Way as New Road!

The Red Lion is a charming half-thatched, half-tiled building, its thatched end being some 100 years older than its tiled end and an original alehouse dating from 1683. Later it was converted to a cottage and the inn was built alongside it. Now the present owners have incorporated the cottage and its garden to good purpose to make the flagged bottom bar with wooden benches and plain tables, a huge fireplace, a multitude of dark beams, a dartboard and a shove-ha'penny board. Beside a huge, dark-oak high-backed settle is a fruit machine. The public bar also has a flagged floor, plain furnishing and a large fireplace opposite the commodious bar area. Across the doorway is the carpeted lounge bar and, up two or three small steps, is the snug, a delightful room under the roof with dark beams and small thick windows. In the corner is a tall Georgian cabinet filled with antique china. Here is the kitchen from where the owner's wife prepares and dispenses the excellent home-cooked food. Each day a curry is prepared with freshly ground spices; this may be of lamb, beef or chicken, and a vegetarian curry is also offered. There are the staple jumbo sausages and steak and kidney pies made with delicious short crust pastry. Sometimes there is smoked mackerel fillet and other times garlic sausage. The sandwiches are very generously filled and are made with thick or thin bread, granary or white. Meals are served at lunchtimes and in the evenings except on Sundays when, in the evening, only sandwiches are offered, a service primarily for the many fishermen who haunt the canal banks.

There is an enormous variety of wines, all of which may be bought by the glass or the bottle, and also several vintage and special ciders. Of real ales there are five on hand-pump: Hook Norton, Morrells Varsity, Wadworth 6X, Bass Bitter and Fuller's London Pride. The very pretty garden is reached from a grassy bank at the back. There are bright flower beds and shady trees and, on the lawn, a good number of picnic benches and tables. Opening hours are from 11 am to 3 pm and 6 pm to 11 pm and on Sundays from 12 noon to 2.30 pm and from 7 pm to 10.30 pm.

Telephone: 0296 668366.

How to get there: From Aylesbury on the A41 toward Tring, turn left at the roundabout in Aston Clinton on to the B489 signposted Marsworth and Ivinghoe. Go straight across two roundabouts into Marsworth village and turn left into Vicarage Road, at the village hall, set amidst a group of trees. The Red Lion is about ⅓ mile on the right of this attractive road, past the church on the left.

Parking: The pub has a large car park.

Length of the walk: 3 miles. Map: OS Pathfinder 1094 Aylesbury and Tring (GR 918147).

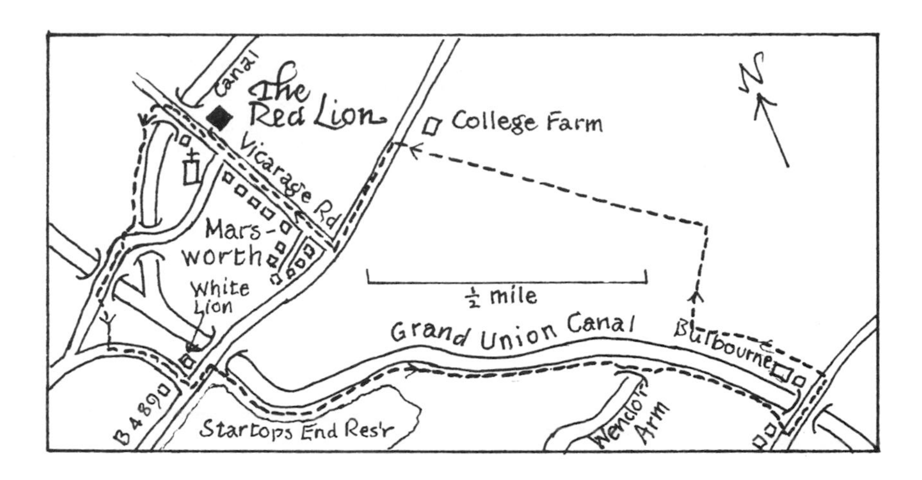

Like Toad and Ratty most of us find 'mucking about' by water irresistible and this walk offers both a quite busy stretch of the Grand Union Canal and the wide, peaceful vista of the open water of Startops End Reservoir.

The Walk

Turn right out of the pub and walk over the narrow hump-backed bridge and descend to the towpath on the left. Follow this for about 400 yards alongside colourful narrow boats moored to the bank; some of them have a veritable garden of flowers and vegetables growing in pots and boxes on their roofs. At a bridge where the towpath ends on this side of the canal at Marsworth junction, go up to the road and across it to walk for about 100 yards along a very narrow little lane, over another humpy bridge with a view of three locks descending, to turn left to cross a field to a gate in the far right corner. Here pick up the lane again and follow it to a T-junction where you turn left on to the busy B489 to walk along it from the Anglers Retreat to the White Lion to take a marked path on the right opposite the pub. Go up the steps on the right to walk beside Startops End Reservoir which is now a world-famous reserve for wildfowl of every sort, from the humble coot to swans and herons.

At the next lock bear left off the embankment to follow the towpath. The tall chimneys of the now defunct Pitstone Cement Works are ahead and the high wooded Chiltern Hills are beyond on the left. Go over five more locks to Marsworth Top Lock and the signpost to the tiny Wendover arm of the canal. Shortly there is a pleasantly laid-out picnic area on the right and, very soon, on the left, Bulbourne Works appears with its quaint brick and tile tower surmounted by an ornate weather-vane. On the water between the house and the works is a bed of large, flat water-lilies, pink and white flowers in abundance in summer and under the leaves live a pair of vast pike who rear up to the surface from time to time and rattle the leaves ruthlessly.

Get up on to the road at the next bridge and turn left to cross it, keeping well in, and walk for about 30 yards to a well-concealed public bridleway on the left. Follow the now well-defined track between tall poplar trees with the works and canal on the left and the gravel pits and old working of the cement works over a high wire fence on the right. The site is now a nature reserve, the exposed chalky surfaces being a natural magnet to a variety of butterflies and the water to a myriad of bright blue dragonflies. Chalk-loving weeds inhabit the edges of the disused pits. The track bears left after about ¼ mile and then you turn right to follow the fence, then left between thickset hedges to the road at College Farm. Here turn left and cross the road to walk on the pavement for the right turn into Vicarage Road by the village hall, then walk up the road to the Red Lion.

9 Brill
The Pheasant

The little town of Brill stands prominently on a hilltop 600 ft above sea-level. The houses coil round the hilltop connecting the common to the pretty square and the wedge-shaped green where the church of All Saints lies hidden behind a thick yew hedge. The common was quarried for clay until the end of the 19th century and there were, at one time, seven local potteries busy making tiles, bricks and rough garden pots. Sheep-grazing on the common is a right and the villagers protested when it was suggested that the humpy undulations formed by the clay workings should be levelled as it was considered that this would reduce the area of grassland. The windmill on the hilltop, a post mill and Brill's most famous landmark, is dated 1668. It is of black weather-boarding with white sails on timber supports hidden, in 1950, by a round brick base to protect the timbers. From the hilltop there are glorious views over Aylesbury Vale to Calvert and over the Oxfordshire plain to the Cotswolds. On a clear day the belching cooling towers of Didcot Power Station can be seen some 20 miles away.

The Pheasant stands tall at the end of Windmill Street, approached by steps from the street or through the garden. The inn is of 17th century origin and its interior has been thoughtfully modernised with comfortable leather banquettes around plain dark-wood tables grouped around the big wood-burning stove, set in a huge fireplace. Up a couple of steps is the dining area with pleasant furnishings in plain dark wood, the walls decorated with some delightful Alken hunting prints. The view from the dining-room windows is of the mill and the countryside stretching away into the distance. Children are permitted in the dining area and, of course, in the neat rectangular garden set with picnic tables and benches. The inn is very popular, with a brisk lunchtime trade; the service is quick, efficient and very friendly. The spotless loos are at the far end of the bar. Dogs are not permitted on the premises; the owners have three of their own.

There are always three real ales on hand-pump: Wadworth 6X, Tetley and Adnams. Three house wines, a red and two white, are served by the glass and there is an adequate wine list. The inn has an extensive menu of starters and main courses, all at very reasonable prices, and specials of the day are listed on a blackboard alongside another featuring tempting home-made sweets such as cheesecake, black cherry flan and treacle sponge. When I was there, among the specials was a Greek salad with feta cheese, a huge portion of smoked Scotch salmon and prawns and delicious barbecued spare ribs. Bar snacks, all very reasonably priced, included a splendidly generous ploughman's with a choice of cheeses or ham, sandwiches and popular burgers with chips. Vegetarian dishes such as home-made lasagne featured on the blackboard.

Opening hours are from 11 am to 3 pm and from 5.30 pm to 11 pm from Monday to Friday. On Saturday the inn is open 11 am to 3 pm and 6.30 pm to 11 pm and the usual Sunday restrictions obtain. It is closed on Christmas Day.

Telephone: 0844 237104.

How to get there: From Thame take the B4011 through Long Crendon. After 3 miles turn right on to an unclassified lane signposted Chilton and Brill; follow the lane for 2 miles into the village. Bear left through the High Street across the Square and turn left into Windmill Street. The Pheasant is on the left at the top of the street.

Parking: There is no car park but ample space is provided on an area of flat ground just in front of the windmill and this would appear to be the official parking place.

Length of the walk: 3½ to 4 miles. Map: OS Pathfinder 1093 Ambrosden and Waddesdon (GR 653140).

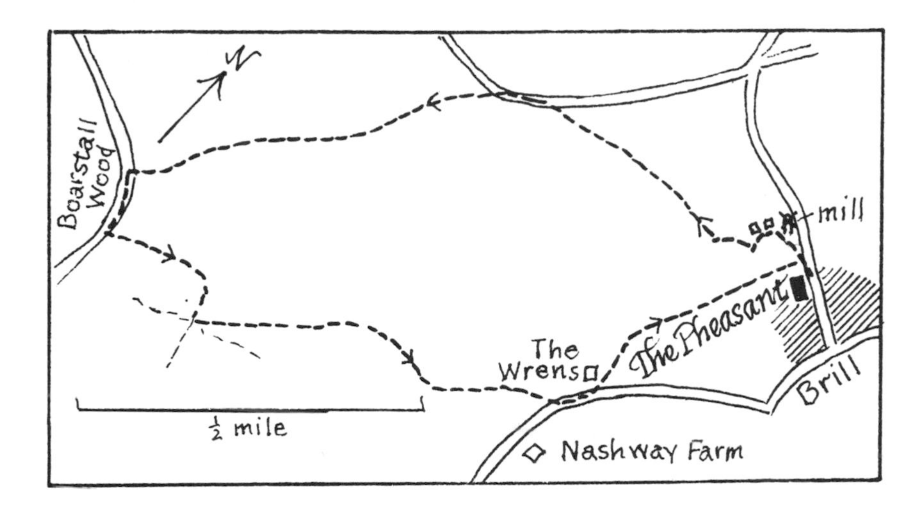

The views on this walk are quite splendid, starting as it does 600 ft above sea-level and dropping to the valley of the river Thame below. The walk is mostly over open fields and these can be muddy at times.

The Walk

Turn left out of the pub and walk toward the windmill; walk on downhill behind it toward a clapboard house lower down. Turn left past it and a very tiny, very old cottage with a crazily loopy-waved roof. Turn right at the junction on to a track for a few yards and bear right past the corner of the cottage with a vine overhanging the garden wall and, after a few yards, into a field to follow the path ahead. After another few yards go over a stile on the left into a large field which you cross diagonally to a stile in the opposite fence. Cross the stile to follow the not-very-distinct path leftward and downhill and cross the ditch ahead by a plank bridge with a large clump of bramble and willow herb to its right. Bear left into the corner of the field to go over the stile on the right and follow the path leftward through a small brake of woodland and on to a lane where you turn left. After about 60 yards or so take the marked path straight ahead away from the sharp right-hand bend in the lane. On the left are two caravans with a small windmill between them; the windmill is used to charge batteries to provide electricity for the caravan dwellers. There are pleasant views of gently undulating countryside all around. Soon the track leads straight ahead on to a grassy and rather overgrown path between high scrubby hedges and squat trees, mostly poplar and oak. In summer moths and butterflies flit about in the tall grasses.

After ¾ mile a road is reached and here turn left to walk along it beside Boarstall Wood on the right and, after about 100 yards, by a bend sign, take the marked bridleway on the left. At the end of a slight incline, go over a broken stile in front to walk absolutely straight ahead across the field with Brill windmill stark on the hilltop skyline on the left and summer larks singing over the ripening crops. Ahead is Nashway Farm.

Go over a small bridge on the far side of the field and then straight ahead uphill over the next field with rabbits scuttling hurriedly back into the thickset hedge on the left. At the top, turn round to admire the wonderful patchwork of fields and wide views stretching away over Oxfordshire and Buckinghamshire to the Chiltern hills beyond. Climb over the high fence at the top of the field and follow the path ahead through a cultivated field, one year bright with yellow rape, next the delicate soft blue of flax growing and interspersed with splashes of scarlet poppies. Work steadily uphill to a T-junction where you turn right to walk on gently uphill to a lane. Turn left here to walk past a handsome house, The Wrens. Just past a sign indicating 'Brill' take the stile on the left into a field and walk straight ahead to a stile on the far side. Go over the stile to follow a narrow little path between a hedge and a fence. Continue, over stiles, along the narrow path and out on to a lane. Here turn left to follow a gravel track and cross the lane at the top to walk uphill by a grassy path to the windmill and the parked car.

10 Cuddington
The Crown

Cuddington is one of the prettiest villages in Buckinghamshire, with an intricate network of narrow lanes interspersed with little greens and long, tall ranks of witchert walls of grey stone or whitewash, thatched or tiled on top, leading between delightful red-brick and timbered cottages in colourful gardens. It has won the Wilkinson Sword 'Best Kept Village' award three times and a hanging sign on one green proudly displays this fact. The church of St Nicholas is Norman in origin but has been much restored and was Victorianised by George Street in 1857. Across the road from it is the charming grey 17th century Tyringham House, which was inherited by the Bernard family of Nether Winchendon, to whom much of the village belongs.

The Crown is a pleasant little pub in the centre of this delightful village and sits firmly at its crossroads. As a result there is no garden, but summery tables and chairs under parasols are set up in the front in fine weather. They vie a little with the small available parking space! Inside is a charming low-ceilinged and beamed bar with a snug off to the side, laid for meals. The furnishings are simple, a great variety of horse brasses decorate the upright beams while pleasant prints cover the walls. A big log fire burns during the winter, and the piped music

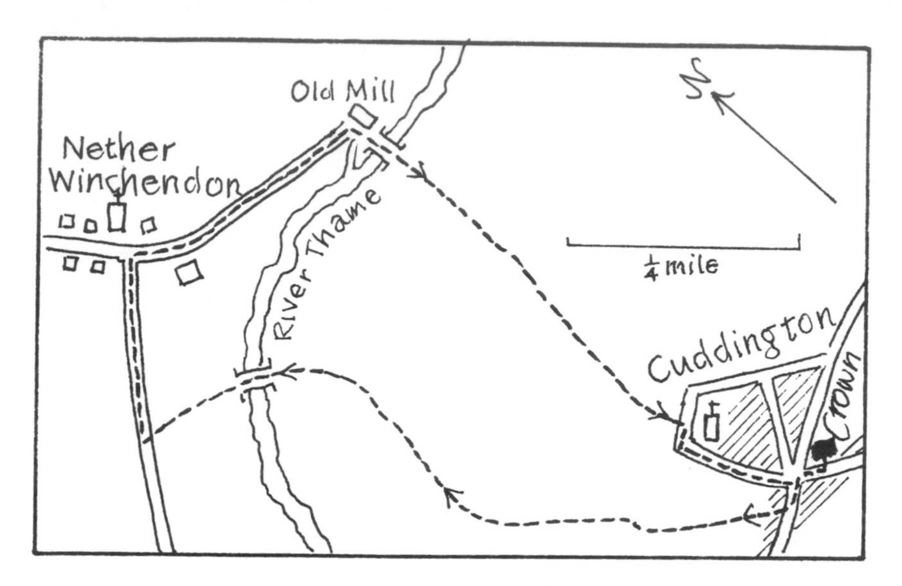

is mostly Mozart and unobtrusive. There is an enormous wine list of both red and white wines of which any may be purchased by the glass or bottle. Real ales include Fuller's London Pride, ESB and Chiswick Bitter, with Scrumpy Jack cider also on hand-pump. Well-behaved children are permitted in the snug. A huge menu board hangs over the lovely old fireplace. Well recommended are prawn vol-au-vents with salad, dressed crab with salad and a crusty brown roll, and, for a hot meal, 'probably the best lasagne in the world'. The ploughman's lunches have a choice of four fillings with a salad garnish; wild boar and Cointreau pâté and Danish smoked trout are both served with hot toast. In winter-time home-made soup appears daily on the menu and there are lots of tempting sweets on the board. Opening times are from 12 noon to 2.30 pm and from 6 pm to 11 pm and, on Sundays, from 12 noon to 3 pm and from 7 pm to 10.30 pm.

Telephone: 0844 292222.

How to get there: Off the A418 Aylesbury to Oxford road at a crossroads is a turning signposted Cuddington, Chearsley and Long Crendon. The village is about 1½ miles down the lane and the Crown is on the right at the crossroads.

Parking: Limited parking space is available at the front of the pub.

Length of the walk: 2½ miles. Map: OS Pathfinder 1093 Ambrosden and Waddesdon (GR 738111).

This charming short walk wanders over tiny streams by plank bridges, goes back and forth all over the small and gently flowing river Thame and passes through the old world village of Nether Winchendon, now bereft of shop and school but possessing a beautiful manor house and mill.

The Walk

Turn right out of the pub and cross the road to the little green on which stands the 'Best Kept Village' sign in front of a pair of pretty thatched cottages and a water pump. Turn right again on to a marked path between magnificent chestnut trees and follow it ahead for about ¾ mile with panoramic views of a wonderfully colourful patchwork of farmland and trees ahead. The path goes over a wooden bridge over the tiny river Thame and to the left is a beautiful stone bridge in the grounds of Nether Winchendon House.

The path emerges on to a lane where you turn right to walk through the hamlet of Nether Winchendon between charming little colour-washed cottages and farmhouses linked by chestnut, ash and sycamore trees and old stone walls. At the junction of three lanes is a small triangle of grass on which stands a Victorian pillar-box and, behind it and to the left, is the church of St Nicholas whose interior is delightfully unrestored, still with high boxed pews and a three-decked Jacobean pulpit. If you are lucky enough to find a 'holy duster' or a flower arranger at work inside, the church is well worth a few

moments of closer inspection. The clock on the front was installed in 1772. A gift of the lady of the manor and unique in that it has only one hand.

Turn right at the junction into a no through road which winds its way past the manor, Nether Winchendon House, the seat of the Spencer Bernard family since the late 18th century and a fine example of an Elizabethan manor house. The house and gardens are open to the public in the afternoons throughout the month of May and occasionally by private arrangement. Turn right again past the front of the Old Mill and go over a stile and a bridge to recross the Thame and on, over three fields, keeping the hedge and a tiny deep-running stream on the left.

At the end of the third field the path crosses the stream by a small wooden bridge with a charming little duck-pond in a garden on the right and a pretty little stone bench by a well on the left. Walk up the lane beside Tibby's cottage and garden. At the top of the lane turn right past Tyringham House, past the side of the church, the school and Bernard Hall, a pseudo-Tudor building on the right and a delightful all-purpose post office cum general stores on the left to the crossroads and the Crown again.

11 Long Crendon
The Chandos Arms

Old and new are inextricably mixed in the village of Long Crendon which certainly justifies its name of Long! The picturesque architecture of much of the village, divided into 'ends', is unsurpassed in the county. The 'ends' represented groups of cottages in huddles removed, very often, from the main village centre and each involved in some particular craft or industry. Lace and needle-making were two such and the courthouse at the far end of the High Street, now in the care of the National Trust, was the staple hall for the storage of wool. The manor of Crendon, given by William I to Walter Giffard, Earl of Buckingham, became the centre of a great park for 'beasts of venery'. The remains of the park and the tall roofs and chimneys of the restored manor house can be seen on the walk.

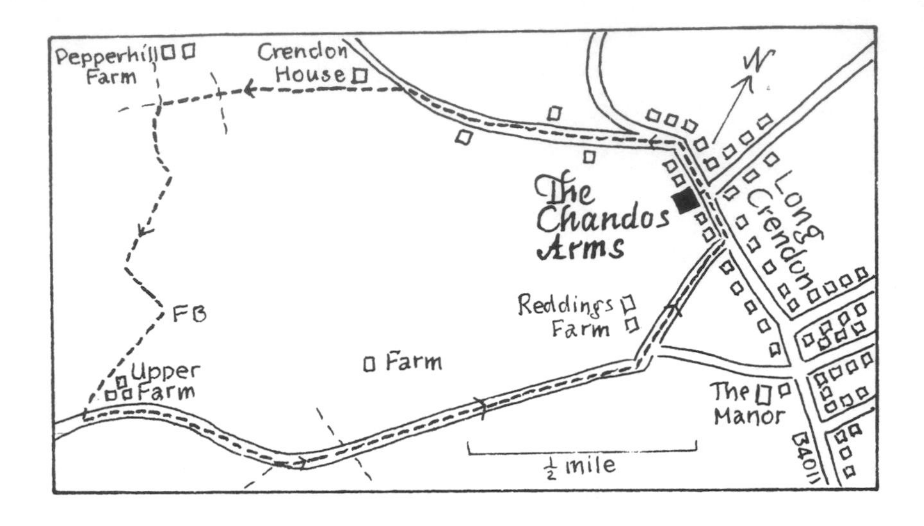

The Chandos Arms, a thatched tavern dating from the 1670s, lies at the north end of the village on the Bicester road. It sits in a little hollow off the road on the left with a small patch of tended grass outside its front door. Beyond the car park is a pleasant small garden with some white garden furniture and wooden picnic tables and benches. Through the low-beamed door is a pair of communicating bars with a small quieter eating area off them on the left. The floor is carpeted and the whole is plainly furnished with wood settles upholstered with red cushions and wheel-back chairs around plain dark-wood tables. The atmosphere is homely and cosy and the welcome from the landlady warm and cheery. At one end of the bars is a huge, very old fireplace and a multitude of brass and copper ornaments decorate the cross-beams and a pretty display shelf. There are no facilities for children but, if eating and well-behaved, they are permitted into the bar and, of course, the garden.

Real cask ales on hand-pump are Boddingtons, Brakspear and Wethered bitters and, as the bar-keeper remarked, a 'gassy' Flowers ale. One red and two white wines are sold by the glass and there is a useful wine list. The menu is large and competitively priced. The eight main course meals include steak and mushroom pie, chicken dishes, scampi and, an unusual twist, Yorkshire pudding portion filled with beef. There are salads of beef, ham or prawns. The ploughman's lunches, various sandwiches and very tasty filled baps are all extremely reasonably priced. Opening hours are from 11.30 am to 3 pm and 6 pm to 11 pm. The usual restrictions obtain on Sundays.

Telephone: 0844 208659.

How to get there: Follow the B4011 from Thame towards Oakley. Three-quarters of the way through Long Crendon village and down a slight incline, the Chandos Arms is on the left.

Parking: There is a sizeable car park to the right of the pub.

Length of the walk: 4½ miles. Map: OS Pathfinder 1117 Thame (GR 688091).

This undemanding walk – no hills till the very end – offers wide views over the Vale of Aylesbury and follows fields towards Shabbington village, high on the next hilltop. The return is made along a peaceful country lane; the last half-mile or so steeply uphill into the village of Long Crendon again.

The Walk

Turn left out of the pub and walk down the road and fork left at the turning for 'Westfield Only', passing a number of charming old cottages and houses in pretty gardens on the way. There are superb views from here over the Vale of Aylesbury backed by the wooded ridge of the Chiltern Hills to the left. Walk past Chaundy's Farm and Bailey's Farm, both on the right and soon notice the intricately patterned brickwork on the face of Crendon House ahead.

Just before reaching the house turn left to go over a stile and along a narrow little path beside the handsome garden. Go over the stile at the end of the path to walk round the field edge with the hedge on the right and, below it, in a deep ditch, a noisy little brook. Follow the path ahead through a gap in the hedge, ignoring the cross path and, at the next intersection, turn left to walk straight across the field ahead and through the hedge. Here bear slightly right to cross the next field to a small gate. Go through the gate and cross the next field and, at the hedge, turn left to follow the path alongside the high hedge on the right and another busy little stream in the ditch alongside it. The village of Shabbington can be seen on a rise to the right over the fields.

After 200 yards or so turn right over a wooden bridge and walk up the field ahead, bearing right at a gap in the hedge just before the yard of Upper Farm is reached, to follow a flinty track round the barns and out on to the road. In summer the song of the skylark may be heard over the fields and kestrels hover and swoop on their tiny prey. The high hedges are bright with may blossom, dog-roses in summer and heavy with blackberry tangles in the autumn. Everywhere there are wide, peaceful views.

Turn left on to the road and walk down it for nearly 2 miles. Brill village stands out on its stark 600 ft high hill on the left while the gentle valley of the river Thame lies quietly on the right over the meadows. The high Chiltern escarpment stands proudly ahead with the tall telephone tower on Kingston Hill to identify it. Keep to the left at the fork in the lane to walk steeply uphill past Redding's Farm to the main road again. Here turn left to walk along the pavement past the Angel Inn and a terrace of delightful little 17th and 18th century cottages to find the Chandos Arms in the dip beyond. There are glimpses through the trees, just by Redding's Farm, of the manor house roof and its twisted chimney pots.

12 Wendover
The Red Lion

Wendover is a pretty little town whose centre still preserves much of its 17th and 18th century building. The quaint clock tower is a 19th century folly, and on the left side of the Tring road lies a row of thatched cottages which were part of Henry VIII's marriage settlement with Anne Boleyn – these are, naturally, called Boleyn Cottages. John Hampden, of 'ship money' fame, and Edmund Burke were both Wendover parliamentary representatives in 1623 and 1796 respectively. The ill-famed 'Hanging' Judge Jeffreys stayed at Wellwick House on his way to assizes at Aylesbury.

The Red Lion was first licenced in the early 16th century, the inn being a major coaching point for travellers from London to the Midlands and Buckingham. In the 1880s a two-horse coach plied daily from the inn to London, offering as reliable a service as could be found at that time for the rather hazardous journey. The profusion of oak beams and inglenooks give an indication of the inn's Elizabethan origin and polished wood panelling and beams are a feature of its bar, restaurant and coffee lounge where a huge fireplace fiercely consumes logs. The inn has hosted many famous visitors, among them Oliver Cromwell, Robert Louis Stevenson and the poet Rupert Brooke. The atmosphere is relaxed and friendly and the service courteous and efficient. The pleasant dining-room is light and airy and the coffee lounge, which is entered from beneath the tall archway, the coach entrance, is furnished with leather and red plush upholstered settles and chairs set around commodious tables; it provides a large dining area for bar snacks or restaurant food, and perhaps a more comfortable ambience for eating than in the bar. The main bar is furnished in the same way and, off it, is another small non-smoking dining-room, the Buttery. The inn has no garden.

Real ales on hand-pump are Marston's Pedigree, Courage Directors, Morland and Brakspear and from time to time there are guest ales. There is an impressive display of malt whiskies behind the bar. Wines, three white and one red, are served by the glass and the inn has an extensive wine list. Specials of the day appear on blackboards both outside and in; they include chargrilled steaks and pork escalope and grilled local trout. The enormous menu of home-made starters and main courses is very reasonably priced as are the tempting array of sweets. Bar snacks feature Red Lion Specials which include venison and home-made chicken and leek pie and some fish dishes. There are a number of fillings for jacket potatoes and ploughman's lunches are served with an assortment of cheeses, ham, and home-made liver pâté, which is delicious. Very good value is the smoked salmon platter, a huge plate of fish in a fluted pattern with salad and served with crusty bread and lots of butter. The inn is very popular both locally and as a venue for travellers, so it is advisable to arrive in good time. Children are allowed in the coffee lounge, the restaurant and the Buttery but not in the main bar. Opening hours are from 11 am to 11 pm every day except Sunday when the bar opens at 7 pm and closes at 10.30 pm.

Telephone: 0296 622266.

How to get there: On the A413 between Amersham and Aylesbury, Wendover High Street is a right turn from the London road at a roundabout on entering the village. It follows a straight and gentle downward route and the Red Lion entrance, a large, square archway, is about three-quarters of the way down on the right. The inn itself is the largest and oldest building on that side of the street so not difficult to see.

Parking: The inn has a very large car park.

Length of the walk: 3 miles. Map: OS Pathfinder 1118 Chesham and Wendover (GR 868078).

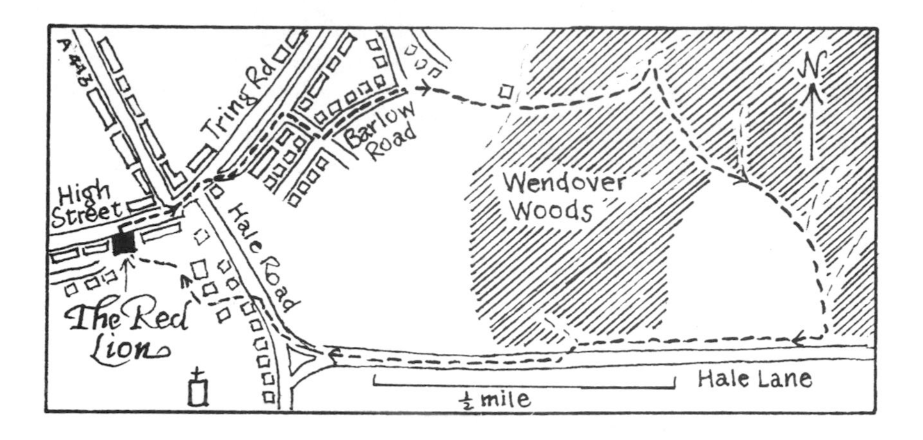

You are spoiled for choice when it comes to walking around Wendover. Having tried this short walk through a part of the Forestry Commission's extensive woodland, you could be tempted to come back again and try another, more open walk.

The Walk

Turn right out of the pub to walk down the High Street to its intersection with Tring Road, in front of the funny little clock tower, now the local information centre. Here turn right into Tring Road and walk past the exit of Hale Road and the lovely 15th century buildings of Bank Farm, set high on a mound on the right. Opposite the farmhouse can be seen the Boleyn Cottages, some of which are still thatched. Bear right at the fork to walk fairly steeply uphill to a turning on the right, Colet Road. Go up Colet Road and turn left at the crossroads into Barlow Road. Follow the road, straight ahead, for about ¼ mile with views of the woodland ahead, and on to a gravelled track.

Bear right at the gate of a house to follow the track ahead to a broken stile leading on to a wide bridleway. Cross the bridleway and take the marked track opposite. Walk ahead steeply uphill through dense mixed woodland, softly green in the spring, shady in the summer and magically colourful in the autumn. There are glimpses here and there of the buildings of RAF Halton far below on the left. Near the top of the hill there is evidence of a Forestry Commission Exercise Trail on the right and the trail itself is crossed close to the end of the track. At the T-junction at the top of the track turn left to walk the few yards to a stile and barrier. Cross the stile and turn right to walk past a little triangle of grass to a broad track beyond another wooden barrier. Go round or under this to follow the track ahead and downhill, ignoring all side turnings, with magnificent views to the left and ahead of the huge wooded bowl in which Wendover lies and, to the right, glimpses of sensually curving fields rolling away. At another barrier/stile go over the stile on to a narrow path between the huge field on the right and the wood edge on the left. Follow the path downhill to a track leading on to narrow Hale Lane.

Just on the corner, where the track meets the lane, there is a stile on the right. Go over this and turn right to follow the path parallel with, and very soon above, the lane keeping the hedge on the left.

Go over stiles and fields and through a small woodland brake where badger tracks bisect the path, descending through the trees to the badgers' feeding-ground across the lane. Go across a small paddock below a rather grand house standing high in parklike grounds and, by stiles, across the drive to the house, Picket Piece. Go over another small field to a pedestrian gate and, after a few yards ahead, there are steps up on to the forest track where you turn left to walk down to Hale Lane again. Turn right to follow the lane down and uphill with pleasant houses set back in huge gardens on the left, open farmland on the right and ahead the green slopes of Coombe Hill, a narrow strip of trees outlining the ridge and clumps of small trees about its grassy fields where horses and cattle graze. Aylesbury Vale curves gracefully round to enfold the whole landscape.

At the T-junction with Hale Road, cross with care and turn right to follow the pavement for a few yards to a marked path on the left, up a steep grassy bank between houses. Follow the path as it meanders steeply downhill between a small paddock on the left and a splendidly tall and thick beech hedge on the right. Over the stile the path leads between attractive gardens to a bridge over a tumbling stream and, over it, on to Heron Path. The path ahead was once used as a rope-walk when rope-making was a local industry in Wendover. The strands of rope would be stretched and plaited walking backward as the plaiting progressed. Turn right to follow the path, crossing the intersection of Dark Lane and on, past Bucksbridge House with the stream still tumbling along on the right. Soon after a bridge across the stream leading into a small housing estate and a grassy area with seats, both on the right, there is a path leading off to the left which takes you straight into the car park of the Red Lion.

13 Worminghall
The Clifden Arms

Worminghall is a small village on the edge of Oxfordshire and its little grey-stone 15th century church of St Peter and Paul is almost inaccessible from the village as it lies in the meadows surrounded by trees, and its entrance is over a cattle grid! At the end of the main street is an unusually handsome H-shaped group of almshouses with stone quoins and mullioned windows founded by John King in 1675 in memory of his father Henry, Bishop of Chichester.

The creeper-covered Clifden Arms lies on the south-west edge of the village and is a truly picturesque black and white thatched 16th century pub. It is at the end of a no through road, surrounded by fields and, rampaging round the pub, a delightfully colourful garden. Ample picnic tables and benches are set out under the trees in the orchard, and there is an ancient, now unused, well and pump. Inside, having ducked your head to avoid hitting it on the low lintel of the crazily hoisted doorway, the cosy little lounge bar has a host of heavy oak beams from which hang a veritable treasure-trove of bottles, brass, powder-flasks, milk yokes, vices and other tools. It is furnished with old-fashioned cushioned seats, some set near the huge fireplace which burns logs fiercely on winter days. The small public bar is uncarpeted but beamed and snug and has a fireplace. The cheerful landlord manages both bars from a small cubby-hole between the tiny counters. Beyond the public bar is a small prettily furnished restaurant. The landlord and his wife offer a warm welcome, and the cooking is good. Real ales on hand-pump include Adnams Broadside and Hook Norton. There is also a dry Strongbow cider and Guinness on hand-pump and a large and varied selection of malt whiskies, one called The Pig's Nose! The wine rack has an authentic dusty look to it and the wine list is small but varied. Three house wines, a red and two white, are served by the glass. Children are welcome in the eating area of the bar and the restaurant and have their own menu. There is a splendid play area at the end of the orchard with a number of grotesque figures to climb through and over.

The food is all prepared and cooked on the premises. Specials of the day appear on a small board by the bar. The food is plain, no-nonsense, sensibly priced and good. Specials can include curried pork, a vegetable lasagne, cod fillet served with proper chips and a good warming soup. Bar snacks include jacket potatoes with a choice of seven fillings, sandwiches with a variety of six fillings and salads. Main courses include steaks, gammon, chicken dishes and a fisherman's platter. There are tempting home-made puddings and a variety of ice-creams and sorbets. Opening hours are from 11.30 am to 3 pm and from 6.30 pm to 11 pm. On Sundays the pub opens from 12 noon until 3 pm and from 7.30 pm to 10.30 pm.

Telephone: 0844 339273.

How to get there: From the A418 out of Thame toward Oxford, turn right in the village of Tiddington on to an unclassified road signposted Ickford and Worminghall. On the far side of Ickford village turn left at Peacehaven Farm and follow the road into Worminghall. At the T-junction turn left again and the Clifden Arms lies a short way up a no through road on the left after a few yards.

Parking: There is a large car park at the inn.

Length of the walk: 2½ miles. Map: OS Pathfinder 1117 Thame (GR 639082).

This is a short but very pretty walk over the fields to the little village of Ickford and back across fields behind Worminghall church.

The Walk

Take the path on the right over a stile just outside the pub and follow it straight ahead over two fields and across a little plank bridge. Go

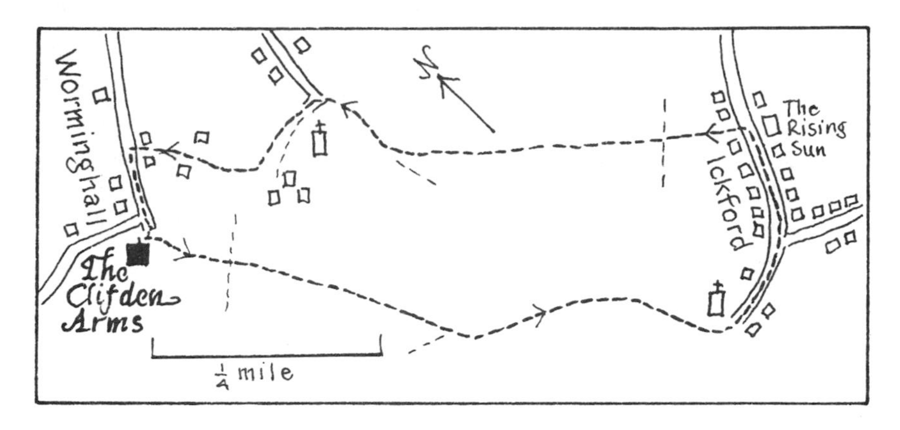

over a stile and then across the next field by a well-defined path. There are magnificent views of the low-lying farmland and the valley of the river Thame which often overflows its banks to create huge lakes of the fields further downstream during long periods of wet weather. The tower of Ickford church is just visible ahead above the trees which surround it. Cross the next field over a stile to another about 50 yards from the left-hand corner of the hedge. The path leads into the churchyard over a small concrete bridge. Follow the path round, keeping to the right of the church of St Nicholas, of 12th century origin, which it is thought replaced a wooden structure of Saxon times. Characteristics of the Norman architecture of the present church are its round arches and windows and the stone string-course running round the chancel, inside and out.

Fortunately for Ickford, its charming church escaped the wholesale restoration and Victorianisation inflicted on so many fine medieval churches. It was sensitively restored by J.O. Scott in the early part of this century, retaining most of its medieval features. If there should be a 'holy duster' or a flower lady working inside, it is well worth a stop to see the handsome interior. The pulpit and some of the pews are 17th century but much of the woodwork was, in fact, the work of Canon Vernon Staley, the incumbent between 1911 and 1933. On the wide window sill of the window in the north aisle is scratched the frame for an ancient game called 'Nine Men's Morris', a combination of chequers and noughts and crosses, played as early as Shakespeare's time, with pegs and pebbles.

Having viewed the church, leave by the gate on to a lane. Notice an incredibly old apple tree in a garden on the right: its gnarled roots appear to be standing in mid-air while the trunk has bowed to take root again and give out branches bearing bright red fruits. At the T-junction turn left and cross to walk on the pavement down the village street past delightful old houses on the left and new ones in pretty gardens on the right. Opposite the Rising Sun pub take the marked path on the left and walk straight across the field to a fence/stile and then turn right through a gate to walk down the field keeping the fence on the left. Bear very slightly right at the start of a hedge towards two stiles across a bridge over a cheery little stream. Notice the lovely jumble of farmhouse and barn roofs and buildings all in warm red brick standing out on the right of the path. In the left-hand corner of the next field is an ancient dovecote. Walk across the field from the bridge to a stile in the left-hand corner leading on to a lane. Go on down the lane for a few yards and then take the footpath on the left by the entrance to Court Farm with the church ahead. Follow the tarmacked path and then turn right through a gate to go ahead through several gates to a road. Turn left and walk along the road for about 250 yards to the fork on the left down which is the Clifden Arms.

14 Great Kimble
The Bernard Arms

The area of Great Kimble has been a settlement since Iron Age times and the name of the village is derived from that of the British king Cymbeline who ruled this area in Roman times. In the 13th and 14th century church of St Nicholas is a framed copy of the report of the parish overseers dated 1635, listing the names of those parishioners who refused to pay the 'ship tax' imposed by Charles I. Heading the list is the name of John Hampden, whose later trial for non-payment was one cause of the Civil War, battles of which raged in so much of Buckinghamshire. It is said that John Hampden rode over the hills from his home in Great Hampden to Great Kimble to interrupt the service of matins in the church, riding his horse into the church during the service to demand that the local farmers, mostly his tenants, stand out against the tax.

The Bernard Arms is on the corner of Church Lane, opposite the church, a large, comfortable, fairly modern building, with a very pleasant long garden with shady apple trees down one side and colourful flower-beds surrounding wooden tables and benches. There is a games room where children are permitted, as they are in the spacious and elegantly furnished dining-room. The main bar is large and carpeted and comfortable chairs and banquettes in a subdued pink plush surround small round tables. There are some attractive bird pictures decorating the walls and on the wall opposite the entrance are large plaster models of Tweedledum and Tweedledee and Billy Bunter. In the other corner is a large fireplace where logs are burned on winter days. There is accommodation in six bedrooms all with showers. Home-cooked hot and cold bar food is served both at lunchtime and in the evenings. The bar menu includes mixed antipasto, smoked mackerel fillet and frito misto d'Orly which is a vast assortment of fish pieces prepared either in filo pastry or a batter made with beer and served with a very special tomato sauce. Home-made soup is always on the menu and Traveller's Choice includes a mixed cheese platter, duck liver pâté, salads and vegetarian dishes. Hot meals of venison, beef and ale pie and swordfish are among a huge variety on the reasonably priced menu. The owner is French and shares the cooking with a fellow-countryman. The wine list is enormous with 55 wines for sale by the bottle. Three house wines, two white and one red, are sold by the glass. The cask-conditioned beers include Marston's Pedigree, Benskins Best, Tetley, and Wadworth 6X. Opening hours for the bar are 12 noon to 3 pm and from 6 pm to 11 pm except on Sundays when the usual restrictions obtain.

Telephone: 0844 346172/3.

How to get there: Great Kimble lies on the A4010 about 4 miles from Aylesbury and 3 miles from Princes Risborough. The Bernard Arms is at the top of a rise opposite the large red-brick vicarage.

Parking: The pub has a good-sized car park.

Length of the walk: 2½ miles. Map: OS Pathfinder 1118 Chesham and Wendover (GR 824060).

This walk traverses the fields below the steep scarp slope of the Chiltern hills at Coombe Hill and near Chequers, the country residence of British prime ministers. The walk leads over the now almost defunct railway line to Aylesbury via Princes Risborough.

The Walk

Turn right out of the pub and right again almost immediately into Church Lane opposite St Nicholas church and walk down between pretty thatched cottages; one flint cottage on the left has a well amid its burgeoning flower-beds. At the 30 mph sign take the marked path on the left up a few steps and over a stile to follow the path beside Kimble Manor on the left and a large pond with water lilies growing

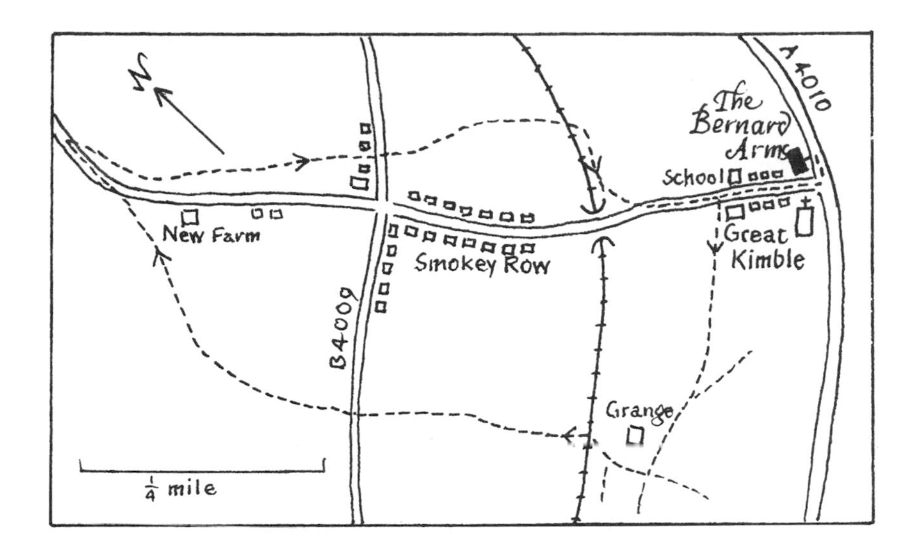

on it on the right. Go through the gate opposite and follow the path straight across the field to a stile opposite and a view of Kimble Grange on the right. Cross the drive to the Grange by two stiles and then cross the next small field to a stile in the right corner. Turn right to walk alongside the hedge to the next stile and go over this to cross the field to a stile and gate by the railway line.

Cross the railway line by stiles on both sides and walk straight ahead over a large field towards a thatched house on the busy road opposite. On reaching the road cross it with care to the track (North Bucks Way) opposite, alongside the thatched house, and keep right along a grassy track between hedges bright in summer with honeysuckle and bramble flowers. After about ¾ mile a lane is reached and here turn left to walk for a few yards to take the marked path on the right with the warm red-brick farmhouse of Kimblewick Farm in a hollow on the left. Walk down the side of the field, keeping the fence and then the hedge on the right and then on across the middle of the huge field. There are panoramic views stretching along the horizon ahead; on the extreme left is Coombe Hill, the highest point of the Chiltern range with its slender Boer War monument on top; below it and backed by dark green woodland is the tower of Ellesborough church, then the stark outline of Cymbeline's Mount with a clump of trees on its bald top, and lastly, Pulpit Hill, so named for its high curving back. During the summer months the air is often shrill with the cries of skylarks whose nests are out of sight in the growing crop.

The path leads over a stile in the corner on to the busy road again and here cross to the path opposite through a little belt of woodland. Follow the path over a stile and into a field and walk across it, keeping the hedge on the left and then over another stile when the hedge will now be on the right to reach the railway line again, crossing this by means of steps, down and up the banks on each side. On the far side turn right to walk parallel with the railway for a few yards and then go up some steps to a little humpy bridge over the line. Turn left to walk up the pretty shady Church Lane again, and turn left at the top of the lane to find the Bernard Arms and the car.

15 Dunsmore
The Fox

There is no better walking country in the whole of Buckinghamshire than the area around Dunsmore, a cluster of gentrified cottages, two pubs and a very small church, perched on a high Chiltern ridge between Great Missenden and Wendover.

The Fox, built in the late 18th to early 19th century, must originally have been the comfortable and fairly spacious cottage of a well-heeled local tradesman. Square and uncompromising, whitewashed and flat-faced with a grey slate roof, it speaks of peaceful and quiet homeliness. It must have become an inn after the Second World War and was run by a quite eccentric lady who always wore a woolly cap and bred dachshunds. The pub, a freehouse, is now a friendly and well-patronised inn.

The doorway of the Fox is reached via the beautiful garden of well-mown lawn and cheery flower-beds and some exceptional flowering shrubs and through a glass conservatory. The long bar faces the door and is very simply furnished with old high-backed settles and dark-wood tables. The floor is of well-worn red flagstones and at one end is a huge fireplae in a deep inglenook where a log fire burns in winter. The conservatory, decorated with a great variety of huge climbing

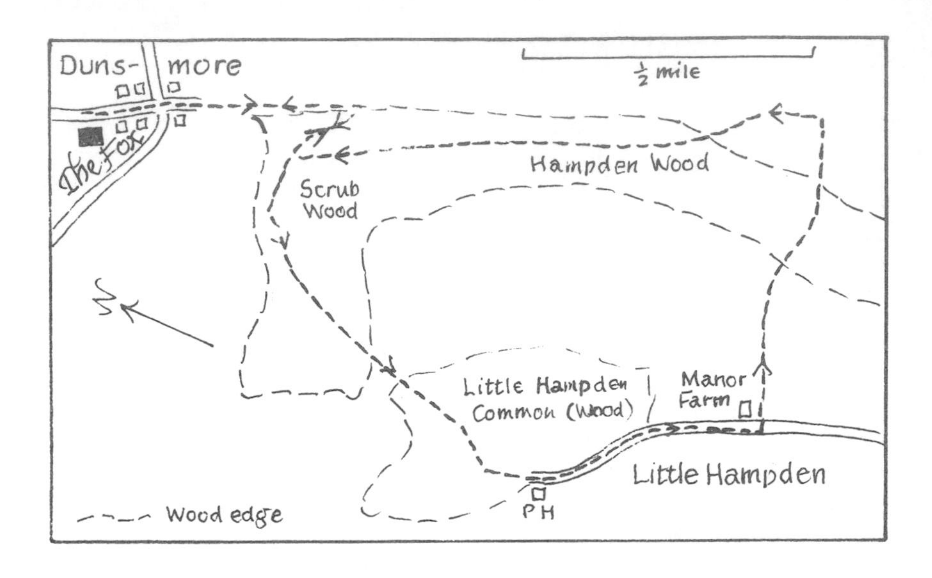

plants in tubs, is furnished as a dining area and well-behaved children are permitted there and in the garden which has a play area and plenty of garden tables and chairs as well as wooden picnic tables and benches. There is always at least one guest ale among the 20 or so stocked, not all on the go at once. Particularly popular and smooth is the aptly named Ridgeway Bitter from Tring Brewery. Also on hand-pump are Wadworth 6X, Adnams, Flowers and Theakston Old Peculier. Guinness and lager are also on hand-pump. Three house wines, two white and one red, are sold by the glass. The menu of specials is on a board in the bar, and there is a good choice of dishes, mostly home-made, from a large menu from which a selection can be made; there are hot meat, fish and vegetarian dishes, delicious home-made steak and kidney pie and a fishy special which is highly recommended. For a snack, a toasted baguette is filled with a generous portion of salad and one of four fillings. All are very reasonably priced. This is obviously a very popular rendezvous so it is advisable to get there early. Dogs must be kept on leads and children *off* flower beds. Opening times are Monday to Sunday lunchtimes from 12 noon to 3 pm, and Tuesday to Saturday evenings 6 pm to 11 pm. The inn is closed on Sunday and Monday evenings. Food is served from 12 noon till 2 pm and from 7 pm to 9 pm.

Telephone: 0296 623186.

How to get there: Along the A413, approximately 3 miles from Great Missenden and 2 miles from Wendover, there is a signposted turning to Dunsmore almost opposite a Jet petrol station. Proceed with care uphill on the narrow, windy lane to a crossroads. Here turn right into an even narrower lane and, after about 150 yards, the entrance to the Fox car park is reached on the left.

Parking: The pub has a huge gravelled car park. As the inn closes at 3 pm and the gates may then be locked, it is advisable to ensure from the landlord that you can retrieve your car before starting on the walk. The landlord is very obliging and, unless he and his wife are out, you will be able to get in. Alternatively, it is possible to re-park the car in the lane close to the Black Horse without obstructing its entry or exit.

Length of the walk: 3½ miles. Map: OS Pathfinder 1118 Chesham and Wendover (GR 863052).

This is a truly lovely walk and not very long but some of the climbing is steep. On very hot days, when walking is thirsty work, there is another pub, the Rising Sun, at the halfway mark on this walk. Muddy boots are NOT permitted in this bar but the welcome is warm and a short break for a drink before the return down and uphill could be most enticing.

The Walk

Turn right out of the pub and walk back along the lane to the crossroads and cross it, with a duck-pond on the right, to walk on past the Black Horse, down a well-used track. After about 400 yards turn right on to a narrow path between wire fences to the high scarp slope of the hill, among wild raspberry bushes, summer foxgloves and dog roses and magnificent views downhill into the richly dark green of the wooded valley and uphill on the far side to wood-edged farmland. In this area a great number of the trees were felled, domino-fashion, in the storm of 1990; their sad gnarled plates of root-systems lie forlornly around but there has been a good deal of reafforestation and the new growth of trees is bright and healthy-looking.

Walk ahead downhill on a tiny path to reach a bolder track at a T-junction where you turn right again to walk quite steeply downhill into the narrow valley. Cross the valley floor, which is often very muddy, to climb uphill on the far side on the well-defined bridle-track through tall beechwoods for nearly ½ mile and then bear left to follow the same track which vastly deteriorates and is muddy most of the time. However, walkers have made a narrow raised 'causeway' to keep out of the mud for most of the route.

The bridle-track ends on a lane opposite the Rising Sun at Little Hampden. Here turn left to walk along the lane for a good ¼ mile past crab-apple and elder trees flowering in the spring on the left, charming small cottages on the right and the tall hills of Great Hampden ahead. On reaching a farmyard on the left, take the waymarked path beside it opposite the little 13th century church where wall-paintings of that date were discovered in 1907. There is a huge clump of honeysuckle winding up a tree at the path entrance. Follow the broad path downhill, keeping the high thick hedge on the left, across the field at the foot of the valley and into the wood again. Turn round just before entering the wood to drink in the spectacular scenery all around and the rosy red brick farmhouse sheltered among shrubby trees.

On entering the wood follow the path bearing left and then right steeply uphill through the wood out into open country and, at a crosspath, turn left over a stile to follow the flinty track along the crest of the hill. Bramble, dog-rose, foxglove, spurge and willow-herb all struggle with wild cherry trees and holly for a place in the inhospitably chalky soil.

After about ¾ mile another stile is reached and, about 100 yards past this, turn up right on to the little path back to the original one between wire fences. At the top of the path turn left to walk along the track, past the Black Horse again to the crossroads and cross over to return to the Fox.

16 Asheridge
The Blue Ball

The tiny hamlet of Asheridge lies along one of the five fingers of hills which run down into the town of Chesham, each divided from the other by a deep, dry valley. There is only one small road through the village and amongst the comfortable farmhouses and small flint cottages, the Blue Ball is comfortably settled and surrounded by a pleasant expanse of green lawn. The atmosphere is sublimely tranquil, the pace gentle and the hurry and bustle of busyness seems light years away from this charming place. Inside, one horseshoe-shaped bar fills the low-ceilinged, beamed space, plainly and unfussily furnished and decorated with colourful poster-type pictures. The landlord and his wife are welcoming and friendly and are kept busy with the lunchtime trade from nearby Chesham. It is a village pub that seeks to serve simple, good home-cooked food at reasonable prices. Food is served at lunchtime every day but Sunday, and is prepared and cooked on the premises.

Specials appear on a blackboard near the bar and include a fish dish, a chicken dish, steak and kidney pie and a vegetarian dish. Four different salad dishes are served and there is a great variety of fillings for jacket potatoes. Ploughman's lunches and a variety of sandwiches

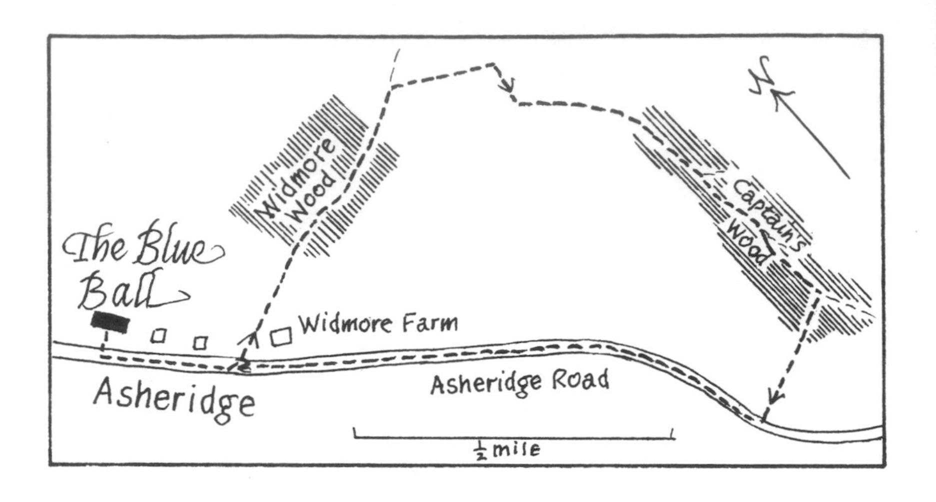

are served with a garnish of salad. Service is very quick and efficient. The games machines are tucked discretely in a corner near the door as are the spotlesss toilets. During summer, weekend barbecues are prepared in the large well furnished garden, where children are welcome.

Four real ales, Arkell's 3B, Fuller's London Pride, Morland Bitter and the very special Morland Old Speckled Hen, are all on hand-pump. There is not much demand for wine but, red or white, it can be purchased by the glass. Opening times are from 12 noon to 3 pm and 5.30 pm to 11 pm and on Sundays the usual 12 noon to 3 pm and 7 pm to 10.30 pm.

Telephone: 0494 758263.

How to get there: From the A416 roundabout in the centre of Chesham, the Asheridge road is a small turning next on the left. After about ¾ mile the road forks, the left fork being signposted Asheridge Road Industrial Estate. Follow this road very quickly passing through the estate to continue up a narrow steep lane to Asheridge village itself.

Parking: There is a very ample car-parking space on the far side of the pub leading into the garden.

Length of the walk: 3½ miles. Map: OS Pathfinder 1118 Chesham and Wendover (GR 937047).

This walk, as one would expect among the 'fingers' of ridges running into Chesham, varies in gradients but none is all that steep and the rewards of wide views over valleys to more lovely wooded hills makes it worth the effort.

The Walk

Turn left out of the pub and, after about 300 yards, take the waymarked path on the left through the edge of Widmore Farm yard and through a gate on the right. Follow the path ahead into Widmore wood which is primarily of beech trees whose tall, greeny-grey trunks stand straight while their branches form a leafy arch overhead. The wood is full of bluebells in the spring as are so many of the chalky beechwoods on the Buckinghamshire hills. Walk gently downhill into a dip and cross a path to walk steeply uphill on the path opposite. After 200 yards or so a broad path is reached running along the crest of the woodland; here turn right and follow the path over a field, keeping the hedge on the left and still walking uphill to the hedge running along the headland.

At the top of the field turn right again and the thickset, obviously ancient hedge is still on the left. In summertime it is bright with dog-roses and elder flowers, wild viburnum whose green berries will later turn to a brilliant scarlet, hornbeam, whitebeam and tall stands of hawthorn, bright pink with heavily scented blossom in spring. Ahead is the richly dark clump of Captain's Wood and, alongside it, the chalky headland is laced with scarlet poppy flowers and the odd left-over of oil-seed rape plant. Soon the path veers leftward for a few yards to continue between the edge of Captain's Wood and a wire fence. High on the right are the houses of Chartridge, yet another of the 'fingers' running downhill into Chesham, and down in the valley are the comfortable fields of Hazeldene Farm.

Soon after entering the wood, take a right fork at a Y-junction of the path and follow the path downhill. Keep right at the next Y-junction to follow the path along the wood edge and, after about 50 yards, turn sharply right down a steep little path above the farm. Follow this path on to a farm track passing alongside the farmhouse and outbuildings.

On reaching the lane again, turn right to walk, quite steeply uphill at first, back along the lane to the pub. Notice the magnificent sweeping views to the left, now down and then uphill towards Chartridge and the gentler slope on the right up to the edge of Captain's Wood, another beechwood carpeted with bluebells in the spring. After about ½ mile or so the pub is reached again.

17 Bledlow
The Lions

Bledlow village is bisected by a deep valley called The Hyde; the manor, owned by the Carrington family since 1801, the 12th century church of the Holy Trinity, some delightful flint and brick cottages of 16th or 17th century origin and the 16th century inn, The Lions, lie near the crest of the heavily wooded Chiltern part of the ancient Ridgeway. The village now incorporates the hamlets of Forty Green, Skittle Green, Holly Green and Pitch Green which sprawl at the foot of the slope while two charming lanes, West Lane and Chapel Lane, join the two parts of the village, through which runs the B4009 almost parallel with the Ridgeway for much of its length. West Lane is proud to have in it the oldest cottage in the village, of old-fashioned 'cruck' or 'crook' construction and called, appropriately, The Cottage. Also in West Lane is a delightful cottage called The City, no one seems to know why.

The Lions stands at the end of West Lane opposite a tiny triangle of grass on which stands a large and solitary tree. The inn's long low-beamed exterior is roofed in tiles which ripple crazily up and down, hither and thither, but seem to stay put to keep out the weather. Colourful hanging baskets decorate the front of the pub in the summer and behind is a small sheltered terrace and a number of small lawns with stupendous views uphill and down. The house has been welcoming walkers for four centuries: nowadays they are asked to remove muddy boots and shoes before entry. The inglenook bar is beamed and furnished with oak stalls built into the panelled walls; other seats and an old settle stand among tables on the polished tile floor. There are huge fireplaces at both ends of the bar and logs burn here during the winter. The food, home-made and freshly prepared, includes a hot soup, filled French bread chunks, ploughman's lunches of assorted cheeses or ham, and a board of special dishes changes daily but retains a home-made steak and kidney pie and a vegetarian dish of the day. Meals are served at lunchtimes and evenings every day except Sunday when there is no food in the evening. Well-kept Courage Directors, Wadworth 6X, Wethered and Young's are all on hand-pump and there is often a guest ale. There is a small restaurant where children are welcome and one of the side rooms has a space game. House wines are served by the glass and there is a good wine list. Opening hours are from 11 am to 3 pm and 6 pm to 11 pm with the usual Sunday restrictions.

Telephone 084 44 3345.

How to get there: From B4009 (Lower Icknield Way) Princes Risborough to Chinnor road, 2 miles from Princes Risborough turn left off the road into West Lane and follow it to The Lions at the top.

Parking: Behind the pub is a commodious car park.

Length of the walk: 3 miles. Map: OS Pathfinder 1117 Thame (GR 776021).

This short walk is full of variety: from the flinty, chalky Ridgeway, bordered by splendid beechwoods, it descends to homely fields and goes through farmyards to return, by country lanes, to Bledlow.

The Walk

Turn right out of the pub and walk toward the church to take a path on the right up a bank between cottages and walk ahead over three stiles and two fields to the Ridgeway. Here turn right again to walk along this ancient chalk track – it may be more than 3,000 years old – ignoring side turnings and through beech woodland bright in springtime with primroses and, later on, bluebells. On the right is a deep dry valley scoured out of the chalky hillside after the Ice Age and now filled with trees of every shape, size and colour; their autumn beauty is magnificent.

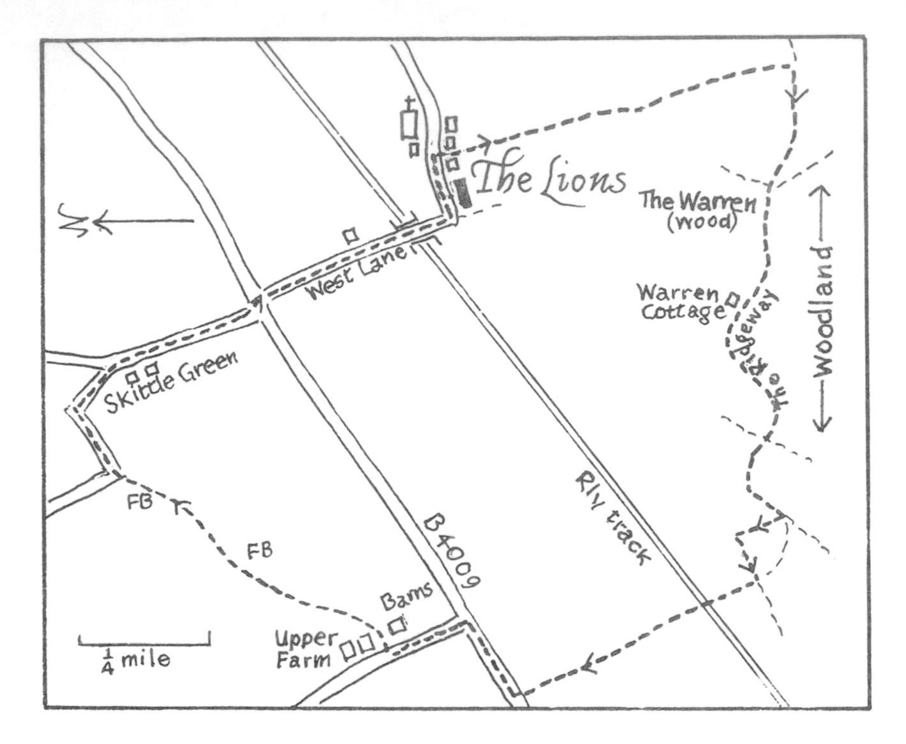

Go past Warren Cottage and then bear slightly right alongside a high thick hedge at a cottage facing down into the valley. Here is Wain Hill Cottage ahead and a confusion of paths; walk forward and take the broadest track leaving Wain Hill Cottage on the right. Follow this bridle-track for about ¼ mile and turn right on to another well-defined bridle-track at an intersection and follow this, bearing left at the next intersection, until the lane emerges, over a railway track, on to the B4009.

Here turn right to walk a few yards along the wide grass verge and then cross to take the lane on the left signposted 'Henton Only'. After 600 yards take a path on the right between high wooden fences just before the entrance of Upper Farm. Go through the wooden gate at the end of the path and bear across the little field to a big metal gate by the farmhouse. This feels like trespassing but the way is marked and the farmer will direct you if you look bewildered! Go through the gate and across the farmyard, keeping the large, modern barns on the right, to go over a stile on the far side beyond a small greenhouse. This will bring you on to what will appear to be a mini-golf course complete with vegetable patch on the left. Cross this to a stile on the far side and then cross the next field to a stile in the tall hedge opposite.

Cross the next field to a metal gate and the next one to a stile over a meagre plank bridge spanning a narrow ditch and cross the next field to two stiles one each side of a broader plank bridge. Over these stiles, cross the field to a large gate opposite on to a lane where you turn right. Walk along the lane, bearing right at the intersection with Holly Green Lane, through the tiny hamlet of Skittle Green to the main road again. Cross with care to walk up West Lane, this time you will be able to admire the lovely hotch-potch of 16th to 20th century houses and cottages before returning to the Lions and the car.

18 Whiteleaf
The Red Lion

The hamlet of Whiteleaf, a dozen or so houses and cottages of 16th to 20th century origin and a pub, the Red Lion, lies along a high Chiltern ridge on the ancient Icknield Way about a mile from Princes Risborough. Carved into the steep, scarp slope of the chalky hillside above is a pre-historic cross, its origins and purpose lost in the mists of time. It has a triangular base with a span of over 26 metres and arms 7 metres wide. It may have been a boundary mark as early as AD 903; it is said to have been, at one time, an arrow-shaped chalk cutting and that the arms were carved out of the chalk later to 'Christianise' a pagan symbol. Most certain it is that the cross is still a landmark, visible from many miles away.

The Red Lion is an 18th century building of red-grey brick and it stands four square, on a slope above the road about halfway along the one lane. Hanging baskets adorn the doorway with bright flowers and the pleasant lawn is set with picnic tables and benches where there are lovely views of the distant hills and nearby thatched cottages. Behind the pub, up steps to the left, there is a large and attractive garden, paved and lawned, and with facilities for barbecues which are prepared on request for special occasions.

The cool and comfortable-looking interior is pleasantly carpeted and furnished with cushioned settles and small tables. On the left of the bar is a small dining-room where children are permitted, as they are in the garden. There is a big fireplace where logs burn merrily in winter.

Cask ales on hand-pump include Hook Norton, Brakspear and Wadworth 6X. House wines are sold by the glass and Guinness and cider are also kept on pumps. The food is excellent, prepared on the premises and astoundingly cheap. On a board inside the bar the specials of the day are listed and include home-made cheese and onion flan with salad, steak and ale pie and fresh cod served with chips and a vegetable. On the menu are basket meals, ploughman's lunches with a choice of cheeses and a generous salad garnish and jacket potatoes with a variety of five fillings to choose from, as well as chicken, meat and vegetarian dishes. Sandwiches are made to order with either brown or white bread and garnished with salad. Service is quick and very friendly. Opening hours are from 11.30 am to 2.30 pm and 5.30 pm to 11 pm. On Saturdays the evening opening is from 6 pm to 11 pm and on Sunday the pub is open from 12 noon to 3 pm and from 7 pm to 10.30 pm.

Telephone: 0844 344476.

How to get there: From Princes Risborough on the A4010 toward Aylesbury, turn right into Peters Lane at Monks Risborough about ¾ mile from the roundabout outside the town. After about 1 mile turn left into the Upper Icknield Way and follow it through the village to the Red Lion on the right.

Parking: The pub's car park is small but limited parking is available in the road below.

Length of the walk: 3 miles. Map: OS Pathfinder 1118 Chesham and Wendover (GR 818044).

Walking a part of the ancient Ridgeway track can be an experience in time-travel, a route of thousands of years; those same ruts and flints on which we stub our toes may have tripped our ancestors many, many times removed from today.

The Walk

Turn left out of the pub to walk back along the road past the delightful mix of brick and timber, thatched, whitewashed and modern houses and cottages to the main road again. Cross to the Upper Icknield Way opposite. This is all part of the ancient Ridgeway track; in fact the word 'Icknield' is so old that there is no known language from which

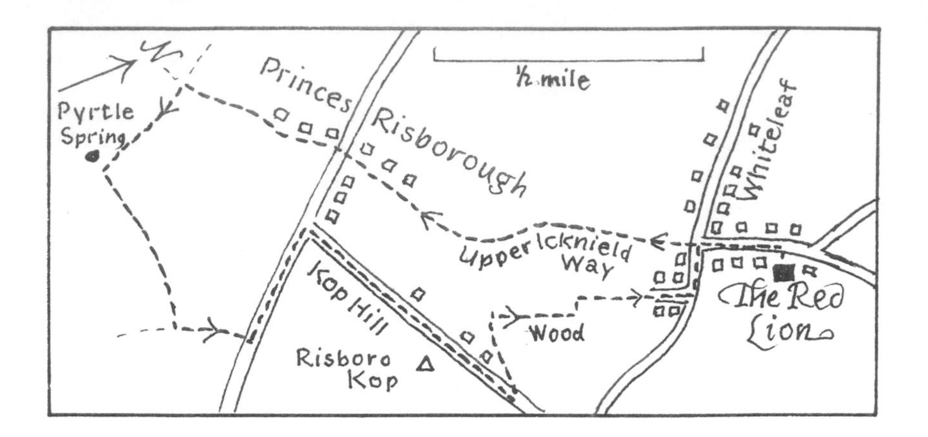

it can be derived so that track must be at least three to four thousand years old. Walking here is indeed walking on history, treading the path, perhaps stumbling over the same stone which impeded the way of an ancestor all of three thousand years ago.

Walk along the shady track, overhung with great sycamore, ash and beech trees and with spectacular views over the Vale of Aylesbury, the tower of Ellesborough church on its mound, and, away in the distance, the Rothschild extravagance which is now the officers' mess of RAF Halton on the right and Bledlow Ridge and Lodge Hill on the left. Ignore all side turnings and soon another crossroads is reached and here cross again to follow the Upper Icknield Way along the contour of the hill for a short ½ mile behind the gardens of pleasant small houses. Soon the trees give way to open countryside with wide views of the hills ahead. At a crossing of the track with two field paths, one on each side of the track, take the left path and walk gently downhill towards Pyrtle Spring, whose origins are also wrapped in mystery, leaving a shadowy pond amid a group of beautiful, graceful trees; nowadays the bed of the pond is often dry. Just past the trees turn left on to a well-defined path along a dip in the undulating field surface with magnificent views of the wooded hills above Green Hailey ahead. Go over a stile in the hedge and turn left to walk up a track to the road.

Turn left on to the road and cross it. Walk along the wide grass verge for a short ¼ mile to turn into Kop Hill, a narrow lane on the right. Walk quite steeply uphill on the lane and, just past the last house on the left and a Buckinghamshire County Council notice about litter, take a path on the left into woodland. Follow the shady, well-defined path through the woods with occasional glimpses of the marvellous countryside below on the left and sunlit patches where scabious plants and flowers are haunted by peacock butterflies.

At a large cross-path turn left as if to follow a path through a gap into, and across a field, then, just before the field gap, turn right to follow the narrow path right along the wood edge to another gap on the far side of the field. Go through the gap and turn left to walk a few yards down the field, keeping the hedge/fence on the right to another gap into an unmade-up road with pleasant houses and gardens on a bank on the right. Walk down the road, Westfield, and turn left at its exit and after a few yards right again into Whiteleaf to walk back through the village to the Red Lion on the right.

19 Ballinger Common
The Pheasant

Ballinger was one of the Buckinghamshire villages famed for their cherry orchards. Children would be sent into the orchards after school to pick the fruit; huge luscious black cherries for jam-making and the noteworthy black cherry pies. These particular trees flourished on the chalky uplands surrounding the little town of Great Missenden, and Ballinger and Prestwood were great rivals for a place of honour as the most delicious pie-makers. Sadly, only a very few of the trees now remain and the famous cherry pies have also passed into history.

Once inside the Pheasant you may well be tempted not to bother with a walk, so warm and welcoming are the owner and his wife and so cheery the atmosphere around the horse-shoe shaped bar. The inn is obviously the central point of life in this small community and well deserves its popularity. Well over 200 years old it replaces a 16th century hostelry which was sited an orchard or two away. The building is of flint and white painted brick with a grey slate roof and stands, square and uncompromising, on a corner. Beside it there is a pleasant patio area with tables and benches shaded with colourful umbrellas. Overlooking the cricket pitch and playing fields is a handsome conservatory which affords dining space for 25 or so guests and where special occasions and parties are celebrated. It is furnished in a restful muted crushed pink colour with rampant climbing plants decorating the walls around the white tables and chairs. The waitress service is charming and efficient. The owners request that muddy boots be removed before coming into the pleasantly furnished bar where cushioned chairs and banquettes surround tables of different shapes, sizes and colours. There is a large fireplace which burns logs in winter and round the walls are lots of charming 'pheasanty' pictures and some plates as well as many copper and brass ornaments. The toilets are spotless; one is roomy and equipped for the wheelchair-bound.

House wines, two white and a red, may be purchased by the glass and there is an excellently discerning wine-list available. There are three real ales on hand-pump: Wadworth 6X, Greene King Abbot Ale and the very specially brewed 'Pheasant at Ballinger' Bitter Ale, the recipe for which is a secret. Cider and Guinness are also kept on hand-pump. All the food is prepared with the best ingredients and home-cooked so the main dishes are not cheap but very good value for money. The menu is extensive and includes duck with a special sauce, venison, halibut and chicken and meat dishes. There are delicious-sounding starters to go with them. The specials of the day appear on a board at the end of the bar and included, on my visit, a splendid leek and ham hotpot, a Ballinger burger of beef with onion topped with grilled cheese in a roll, jacket potatoes with a choice of four fillings, a ploughman's platter and sandwiches of white or brown bread with various fillings. Children are allowed in the conservatory and the bar if they are eating and on the patio outside. There is no play area attached to the inn but the playing field is just a path away opposite the conservatory. Opening hours are from 12 noon to 3 pm and from 6.30 pm to 11 pm. Meals are served at lunchtime from 12 till 2 pm every day and every evening except Sunday from 7 pm to 10 pm. The usual Sunday opening restrictions obtain.

Telephone: 0494 837236.

How to get there: From the A413 at Great Missenden take the B485 at the roundabout signposted for Chesham. About ¼ mile up the very steep hill turn very sharply left and follow this unclassified lane, across the crossroads at South Heath and bearing left as signposted, for about 2 miles. The Pheasant inn is on the left and the car park is down a side track just before the inn itself.

Parking: The inn has an ample car park.

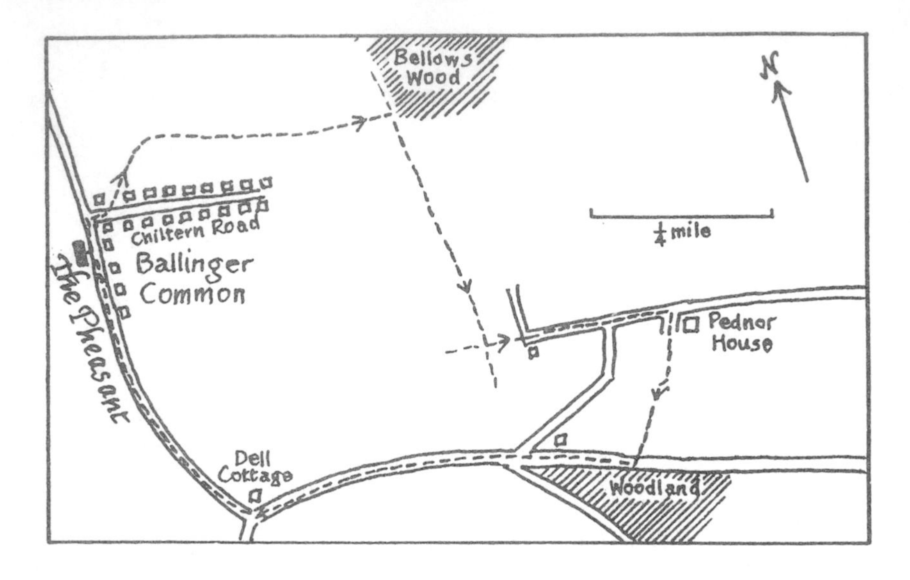

Length of the walk: 2 to 2½ miles. Map: OS Pathfinder 1118 Chesham and Wendover (GR 913032).

This short walk encompasses every aspect of walking in the Buckinghamshire countryside: the blue-grey of the air between tall, greeny-grey beech trunks, wide views sweeping down from hilltop fields and delightful old warm flint and brick cottages and houses and the grandeur of Pednor House.

The Walk

Turn left out of the pub and walk down the lane. Soon turn right into Chiltern Road and left almost immediately on to a footpath between gardens. At the T-junction on the edge of a huge beechwood, turn right and walk along the shady path to a stile into a field. Go over the stile and, keeping close to the hedge on the right, walk across the grassy field to the next stile tucked up in the far corner. In the autumn huge blackberries grow in the hedge and there are sweeping views to the left over the cornfields.

Go over the next stile and follow the path, hedge now on the left, straight ahead and looking out for pheasants, hurrying and gleaning among the stubbly corn stalks. After two fields, a stile alongside a murky pond is reached; go over this one, turn left to clamber over yet another and follow the track straight ahead and on to a narrow lane at a sharp bend. Keep on down the lane past a charming half-timbered 16th century cottage to look at the magnificent Tudor manor of Pednor House, set between four large red-brick pillars. Its courtyard extends back to the warm brick and timbered house with a splendid carved wooden door set in a heavy carved frame and a beautiful barn of the same brick and timber 20 yards long.

Retrace your steps for about 50 yards to take a narrow little path on the left, well hidden in the thick hedge of box and holly. In the spring a huge rhododendron flourishes and its great pink blooms overhang the path while two jolly little black dogs clatter noisily back and forth on the other side of the hedge. At the end of the path, go through an intriguing little metal 'squeezer' and follow the path steeply downhill to another squeezer on to a bridleway where you turn right with woodland on the left and a rolling hillside on the right.

The bridleway soon leads on to a crossing of lanes beside a delightful flint cottage. Walk straight ahead between trees; the beeches, thwarted by pruning from growing tall, have thickened trunks and the grotesquely convoluted branches twist this way and that from their base, forming intricate patterns. Just past flinty little Dell Cottage, at the signpost, turn right to walk uphill through Ballinger Common, past some very attractive houses, some very old and some more modern, set behind immaculate lawns or bright flower-beds, and the little War Memorial Hall of which the residents of Ballinger are inordinately proud and careful, back to the Pheasant and the car.

20 Chesham Vale
The Black Horse

Pleasant walks abound round the outskirts of the little town of Chesham nestling in a valley, the source of the river Chess. To the north, and just out of the town, is Chesham Vale, a gentle wood-capped landscape of arable and corn fields sloping upward towards the ridge of hills on which the hamlet of Hawridge stands.

The Black Horse presents a delightful black and white exterior with a warm red-tiled roof and, in summer, a riot of colourful flowers in tubs and hanging baskets in front of the inn. Behind it is a long, well-mown lawn with plenty of wooden tables and benches and a children's play area at the rear. Inside there are massive black beams and joists to support the low-ceilinged bar with its rough-plastered white walls and huge inglenook fireplace. Behind is another spacious room furnished with dark-wood tables and wheelback chairs, high-backed winged settles and benches cushioned in a pleasant muted shade. The walls are decorated with horse brasses and some sporting prints. The whole presents a comfortable and welcoming air and the service is prompt, friendly and polite. The speciality of the house is its home-made pies, examples of which are beef with Guinness, wild rabbit with tarragon and peppers, pork and apricot, or venison with red wine, all very reasonably priced and of generous proportions. There are seven fish dishes from which to choose, casserole of pheasant, jacket potatoes with various fillings and vegetarian dishes. Much to be recommended are the wild boar, apple and red wine sausages served with 'proper' chips and a vegetable. There is also a home-made soup, ploughman's lunch or fresh filled baguette served with a generous garnish of salad. Three wines, a dry and a medium white and a red house wine, are sold by the glass and there is an extensive wine list, including champagne. Well-kept real ales include Adnams, Benskins Best, Wychwood Best and Ind Coope Burton. Children are permitted in the bar for food during the early evening only when a booking is made.

The inn is open from 11 am to 2.30 pm and from 6 pm to 11 pm and meals and snacks are served every day from 12 noon to 2 pm and from 6 pm to 9 pm except on Sunday evenings. The Sunday opening hours are from 12 noon to 3 pm and from 7 pm to 10.30 pm.

Telephone: 0494 78465.

How to get there: On the A416 from Chesham toward Berkhamsted take the left fork just on the edge of the town signposted Hawridge and Cholesbury. The Black Horse is about 1½ miles up the lane on the left.

Parking: The pub's car park is enormous so there is no risk of obstructing customers if you leave the car while walking, but it is advisable to let the landlord know this.

Length of the walk: 3 miles. Map: OS Pathfinder 1118 Chesham and Wendover (GR 964045).

Typical of the narrow ridges of hills sweeping down into Chesham and the Chess valley are the hills on this walk. The views are wide and spectacular and there are often great splashes of colour made by poppies in the summer fields or willow-herb in the autumn.

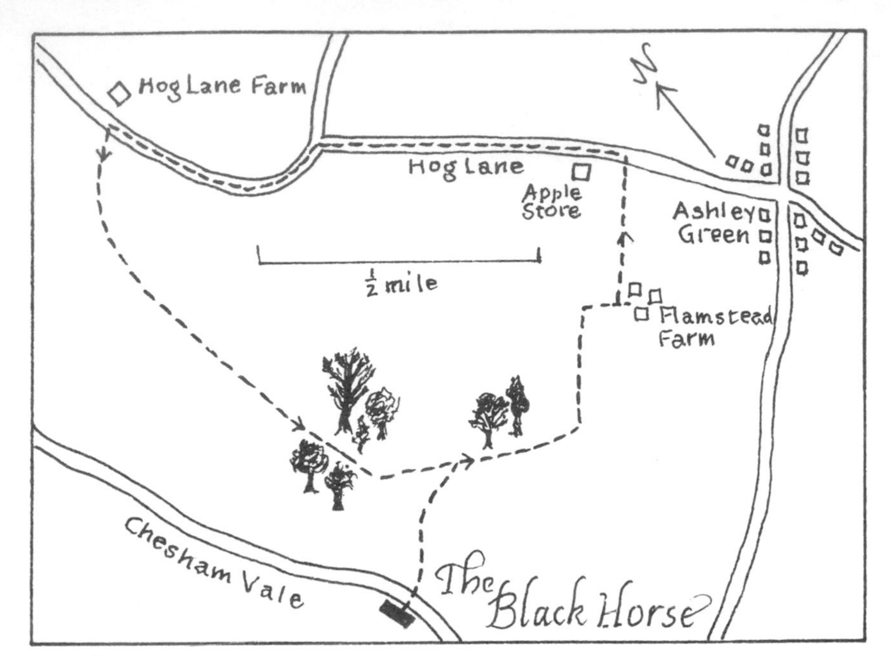

The Walk

Cross the lane to a bridle-track immediately opposite and follow it, walking gently uphill between tall hedges of witch-hazel, dog-rose and blackthorn. After about ⅓ mile the path narrows and winds through a belt of woodland and, after about 400 yards, it turns sharply left to wander on, through a big green gate, to the yard of Flamstead Farm. Turn left across the yard to follow the path, through another green gate, to reach Hog Lane, on the outskirts of Ashley Green in about ½ mile.

Turn left on to the lane and follow it past an attractive farm shop called the Apple Store. There are widespread views of small paddocks and large fields where black and white cattle graze. Turn left again at the T-junction and, after another ½ mile, take the marked footpath on the left through a rickety wooden gate opposite the entrance to Hog Lane Farm. The footpath sign at the kissing-gate next to the wooden one is quite concealed by the overgrown hedge.

Keep to the left of the field and downhill. Go over two stiles, also concealed in the hedge, about 20 yards down and cross the next field to an enormous stile opposite. Go over the stile and cross the field, keeping the hedge on the left, to another stile in the left-hand corner. Bear right here to follow the path along the field edge alongside a tall thickset hedge, crossing a track and following the path ahead over another huge field. There are wide views of prosperous farmland surrounded by woods and, ahead, one huge solitary oak tree in the middle of the field. Just past the tree the path gives a little jink to keep the tall hedge now on the right where willow-herb makes huge splashes of colour in late summer. Over another stile enter a little belt of mixed woodland. Emerge from the wood to panoramic views of the rolling countryside and turn left to follow the path along the field edge gently downhill and over a stile to bear right over another to reach the original bridleway where you turn right to return to the Black Horse opposite.

21 Little Missenden
The Crown

The Crown is a quintessential village inn in a perfect English village and the walk from it is quite beautiful. The inn is 200 years old though it started its life as two cottages which were later joined to make the pub. For 70 years it was run by the same family, the Claytons, and then Mr Clayton's daughter, Mrs Taylor, ran it. The present landlord purchased the freehold from Ind Coope some years ago so that it is now a freehouse. It sits square on the roadside; in summer hanging baskets of lobelia and geranium make brilliant splashes of colour at the front and behind the pub is a long well-kept garden with plenty of benches and tables. The bar is small and snug, the servery in the centre, opposite the door. One end is almost a museum of 19th century farm implements – plough-shares, hooks, flails and so on – while the other end is a picture gallery of old photographs of nearby towns and villages.

Morning coffee is served in the bar as are Hook Norton and Marston's real ales. The menu of bar snacks is fairly limited but very reasonably priced, home-made soup really is home-made and the various sandwiches, of white or brown bread, are freshly prepared and attractively decorated with a salad garnish.

Telephone: 024 06 2571.

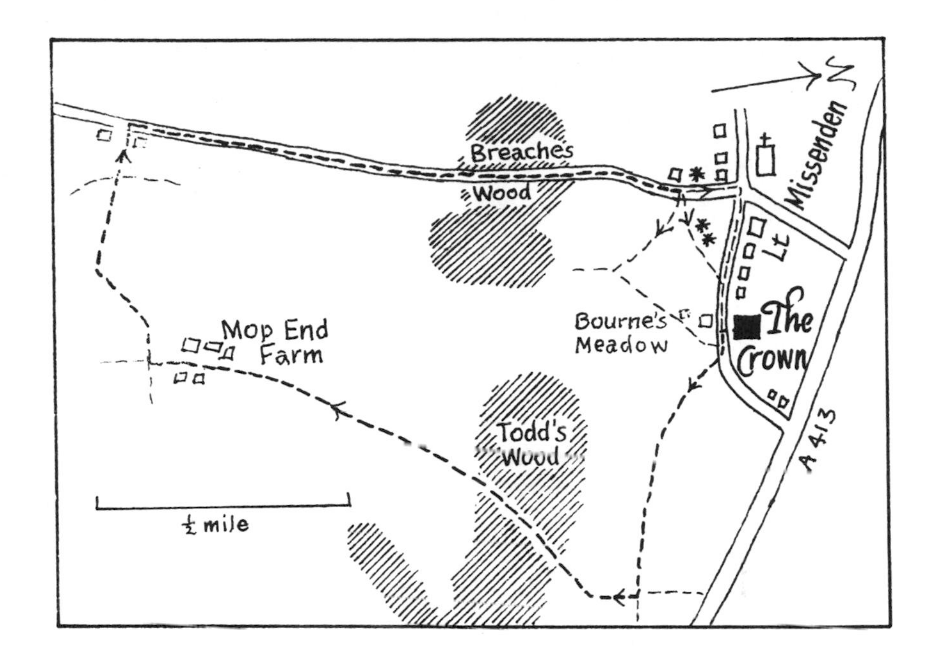

How to get there: Little Missenden is reached from the A413, Amersham to Aylesbury road. From Amersham the turning to the village comes on the left just before the end of the dual carriageway and the end of the Amersham bypass. From Aylesbury, it lies on the right about ¾ mile from a railway bridge over the road just past Great Missenden bypass. The Crown is at the Amersham end of the village.

Parking: There is ample parking space for cars beside the inn and on the far side of the road.

Length of the walk: 3½ miles. Map: OS Pathfinder 1138 High Wycombe and Amersham (GR 922989).

The walk starts along a path in the Misbourne valley but leaves it quite quickly to forge through woodland and uphill to Mop End. Most of the return is made along a quiet country lane between isolated cottages and houses.

The Walk

Turn left out of the Crown and walk down the lane for 30 yards or so to take a marked footpath ahead on a sharp bend of the road. It is signposted South Bucks Way. Follow the track between low tree-capped hills on the right and flat meadows on the left through which the tiny river Misbourne sometimes will deign to flow. Ahead is a farm with a magnificent red-brick and timbered barn. After about ½ mile, go through a gate and turn right on to a track leading gently uphill through some mixed woodland. There are glimpses of sweeping countryside between gaps in the trees on the right. Continue on the flat along the track between high, sweet-scented hedges for a good mile to Mop End Farm. About 200 yards past the farm entrance take a marked path on the right and follow it straight across the middle of the field. Cross the rough bridle-track on the far side by two stiles and cross the field opposite. Go over another stile and follow the path past some cottages for about ¼ mile, turning right on to a lane at the end of the path. Follow the lane gently downhill past pretty flint and brick cottages out into open country and then back again into beech woods.

Below the wood, where another lane enters on the left, the walker has three choices: one, to continue on down the lane turning right (* on map) at the T-junction opposite the fine Tudor manor house to walk back to the Crown through the village; two, to take the path on the right uphill again past a large and solitary ash tree to join a track on the far side of the field – here turn left and follow the track downhill again past Bourne's Meadow to emerge on to the road opposite the Crown; three, to follow the path on the right along the left-hand field edge, hugging the hedge, to come out on to the road through the village a few yards from the Crown back up the road on the left (** on the map). If a visit to the lovely old church of St John the Baptist is desired, turn left at the T-junction and follow the lane for a few yards to the church on the right. There are some interesting 13th century wall-paintings to see.

22 West Wycombe
The George and Dragon

The village of West Wycombe, now in the hands of the National Trust, is dominated by its great hexagonal mausoleum and the church of St Lawrence with its gleaming golden ball on the hilltop, 646 ft above sea-level. The church is medieval in origin and its parish extended as far afield as the hamlet of Downley on the hilltop opposite as well as the settlements around its feet. It now has a Georgian nave provided, in 1765, by Sir Francis Dashwood who also had built the rosewood pews and lectern. The gilded ball on the top was added in 1763, a copy of one on the customs building in Venice. It is open to visitors on Sunday afternoons in the summer. The 18th century Palladian house of West Wycombe Park, with temples and arches, a landscaped park and lake, church, caves and mausoleum are all part of a grandiose landscape scheme invented by Sir Francis who is said to have entertained his friends of the Hell-Fire Club in the caves. These are open to the public in the afternoons all the year round. The mausoleum was erected by Sir Francis in 1762 and the urns in the niches were to contain the hearts of his Hell-Fire friends.

The George and Dragon, an 18th century coaching inn, lies on the A40 in the centre of the village and it is easy to miss the fine but

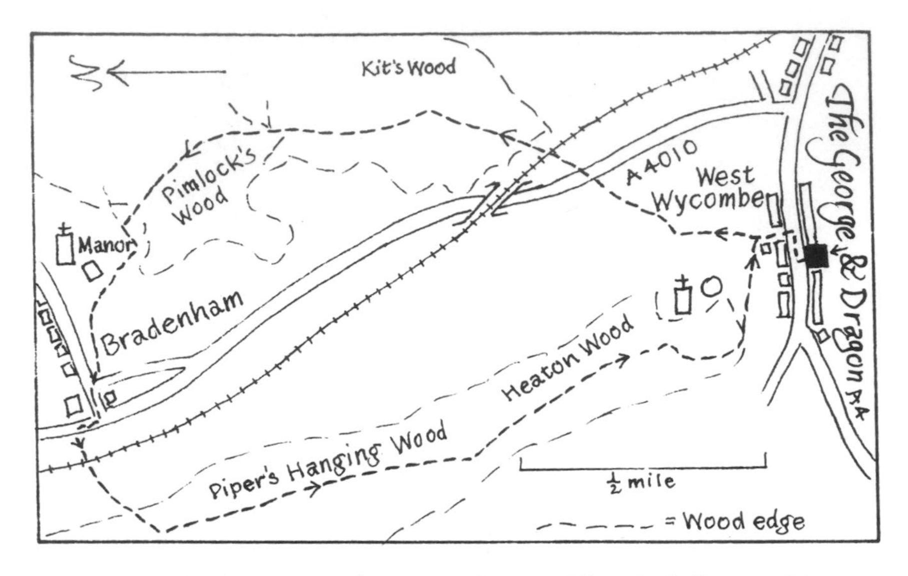

narrow arched entrance between the rambling building and its car park and garden beyond. However there are ample rewards when the entrance has been achieved. To the left, immediately inside the door, is a tiny snug bar very simply furnished with hard-backed chairs and tables and a settle; attractive etchings and prints decorate the walls. The large main bar has massive oak beams, sloping walls and, in winter, a fine log fire burns. From the bar a magnificent oak staircase leads up to the first floor. This is said to be haunted by a wronged maiden. The furnishings are plain and comfortable and the atmosphere cosy and welcoming.

Specials appear on a board behind the bar each day and there is a very comprehensive, though not overly expensive, menu of dishes including home-made pies such as ham, leek and cider or Cumberland sweet lamb, casseroles and fish and vegetarian dishes. Good home-made soup with a chunk of crusty bread is a fine cheap filler on a cold day. Sandwiches of prawn, chicken tikka, cheese and onion or ham are generously filled and the crusty bread really is crusty and deliciously fresh. House wines, a dry and a medium white and a very drinkable red, may be bought by the glass and there is a wine list. Courage Best and Directors and Marston's Pedigree are the real ales always on sale and there is a guest ale, all on hand-pump. Service is quick and pleasant. Opening hours are from 11.30 am to 2.30 pm and 5.30 pm to 11 pm on weekdays and the usual restraints apply on Sundays. Meals are served from 12 noon until 2 pm and from 6 pm to 9.30 pm. Children are permitted in the eating area of the bar. The lawned garden is amply supplied with picnic tables and benches and there is a children's play area at the far end.

Telephone: 0494 464414.

How to get there: Follow the A40 from High Wycombe toward Oxford, bearing left at the Pedestal roundabout to enter West Wycombe High Street. The George and Dragon is about halfway along on the left and the arched entrance is just below the hanging inn sign.

Parking: The pub has good parking facilities beside the garden.

Length of the walk: 4½ miles. Map: OS Pathfinder 1138 High Wycombe and Amersham (GR 829947).

This is a walk with splendid views over deep valleys and across hills but, in order to see the views, you must climb the hills and some of them are quite steep, though the climbs are not very long.

The Walk

Cross the road outside the inn to the splendid hanging clock above the arched entrance to Church Lane and follow the lane uphill beside pretty cottages on the left and a high flint and brick wall on the right. After about 500 yards take the marked path on the right to strike diagonally across the field towards the A4010 in the valley. Cross the road to the path opposite and follow it, carefully, over the quite busy railway line ahead and steeply uphill through Kit's Wood. The carpet of dog's-mercury under the trees announces that this is a very ancient woodland; the plant takes many years to establish.

Follow the broad path through an area where many of the trees were felled by the hurricanes some years ago. Their huge, flat plates of root-systems stand starkly and rather sadly among the hugely tall foxgloves which have taken over. The roots are deliberately left in situ as they provide growing space for small wild flowers and brambles and homes for a variety of insects which, in their turn, provide food for birds and mice. Some reafforestation has been started here. There are splendid views to the left dropping steeply downhill to a clump of small houses and uphill beyond them to the chalky, wood-edged hills toward Bledlow Ridge.

At the fork in the path keep left and follow the path between tall isolated beech trees steeply downhill into thick woodland. The path curves to the right to reach a cross path in the valley bottom where you turn right to follow the path uphill again for 250 yards or so to bear left at a cross path to follow a broad track ahead for about ¼ mile. Look out for a broad white arrow painted on a tree trunk to indicate a narrow little path on the left which you take to come gently downhill to the wood edge and then sharply left at another arrow and steeply downhill to join a bridleway at the bottom.

Turn left on to the bridleway and, in a few yards, the handsome façade of 18th century Bradenham Manor comes into view on the right. This was the last home of Isaac D'Israeli who died in 1848 and was buried in the nearby church of St Botolph. The house is immortalised by his son, Benjamin Disraeli, in *Endymion*. The National Trust took over the village of Bradenham in 1956. The large cricket green dominates the scene. Above it, to the right, are the church and manor and in front is a row of charming flint and brick cottages in colourful gardens and a strange grey neo-Gothic edifice. Cross to the lane opposite over the rough-mown part of the cricket green.

Turn left to walk down the lane to the A4010 which you cross with care to take a marked path between large wooden gates opposite the entrance of Manor Farm and a little to the right of the Red Lion pub. The footpath sign, beside a kissing-gate, has been beautifully obscured by a rampant chestnut tree and a hawthorn. Cross the small field to a stile to cross the railway again and follow the path over the field, through a hedge and over another field where the narrow path leads through long grasses and scrubby bushes of dog-rose and hawthorn to a stile into a wood.

Cross the stile to enter the wood, bright with dog violets and oxalis in the spring and tall pale pink to deep red foxgloves in the summer. The path winds its way through the wood and relentlessly uphill. Stop near the top of the hill to look out leftward over the valley to the village of Bradenham and beyond. Turn left at a T-junction on to a broad track and follow it past Nobles farmhouse and along the edge of the wood for around 1 ½ miles passing splendid views on the right now, downhill through the trees and uphill again towards Booker and Lane End. Suddenly ahead, the golden ball of St Lawrence church peeps coyly out from the trees and then as quickly disappears again.

On reaching the flat grassy car park near the church, turn right to walk across it to the church and then follow the path to the left beyond, alongside its churchyard wall, to see the famous mausoleum. On the right is a panoramic view of the town of High Wycombe with the A40 running straight as an arrow into it.

Follow the grass path below the mausoleum downhill with a grand view of the house in West Wycombe Park across the valley to the right. Follow the path down steep steps overlooking a hotchpotch of red-tiled roofs and colourful gardens to the famous caves and turn left on to the road to follow it downhill past rose-filled little cottage gardens to the arch on to the A40 again. Cross this to reach the George and Dragon.

23 Chenies
The Bedford Arms

Chenies is a typical example of a feudal or 'closed' village pattern. It was greatly expanded and much rebuilt in the agricultural boom of the early 19th century, and a great many of the cottages bear dates in the 1840s. Reputedly the name Chenies derived from the Cheyne family who lived there for many years and owned property in the locality. A parish map on the wall of the bus shelter details all the important buildings in and around Chenies.

The Bedford Arms has a pleasant homely exterior; it could, in fact, have been the home of an 18th century small landowner. It is of warm red brick, tall and square and, in summertime, has pleasant flower-beds and hanging baskets in colourful bloom. On the left is a very attractive garden with a fishpond and more flower-beds and with beautiful views all round from the numerous benches and tables set out on the lawn. A small part of the garden is reserved for hotel guests. Inside is a charming bow-windowed lounge bar furnished in a gentle peachy-coloured upholstery and opposite is a room where children are permitted. The main long bar, carpeted and with heavy oak beams, is pleasantly furnished with upholstered settles and chairs round small tables and there are some attractive prints decorating the walls. The immaculate loos are on the left past the bar; for drying your hands there are individual cotton towels, which are then discarded into a wicker basket for laundering. Service is courteous, quick and efficient.

Hook Norton, Younger's IPA and Theakston Best Bitter real ales are on hand-pump and there is also Dry Blackthorn cider. The wine list is large and comprehensive, mostly for the restaurant, but three house wines, a red and two white are served by the glass. There is an attractive restaurant where à la carte meals are served. Specials are listed on a board in the bar and include avocado and asparagus salad, beef Stroganov and grilled salmon. The huge menu includes steak and Guinness pie, chicken dishes, scampi, tagliatelle, sausages and burgers and a huge cold buffet. Jacket potatoes are offered with a choice of five fillings and sandwiches with fillings such as ham and Gruyère, roast fresh turkey and crab are very reasonably priced. All food is home-made and prepared to order.

Telephone: 0923 283301.

How to get there: From the A404 from Amersham, go through Little Chalfont and take the third major turning for Chenies on the left and follow the road for about ¾ mile to find the Bedford Arms set back a little on the right.

Parking: Beside the pub on the right is a sizeable car park and a large grass paddock is used as an overflow.

Length of the walk: 2½ or 4 miles. Map: OS Pathfinder 1139 Watford and Rickmansworth (GR 018984).

This is a short but truly delightful walk which can be lengthened if desired. It encompasses farmland, woodland and lovely stretches alongside the little river Chess and its watermeadows.

The Walk

At the far side of the hotel car park is a gap in the hedge which leads down three steps on to a lane. At the lane turn right to walk along the drive of Mountwood Farm with superb rolling views to the left down and uphill over the Chess valley. Bear right before the farmhouse on to a grassy path off the main drive and, immediately past the farm buildings, go over a stile on the left and across a small field into Mountwood. Here are magnificent views of the wooded hills on the far side of the deep river valley through the trees. Follow the path downhill through the wood to a stile on the right which you cross to follow a narrow path along the wood edge, with open views of paddocks and new plantation, to another stile at the bottom of the hill.

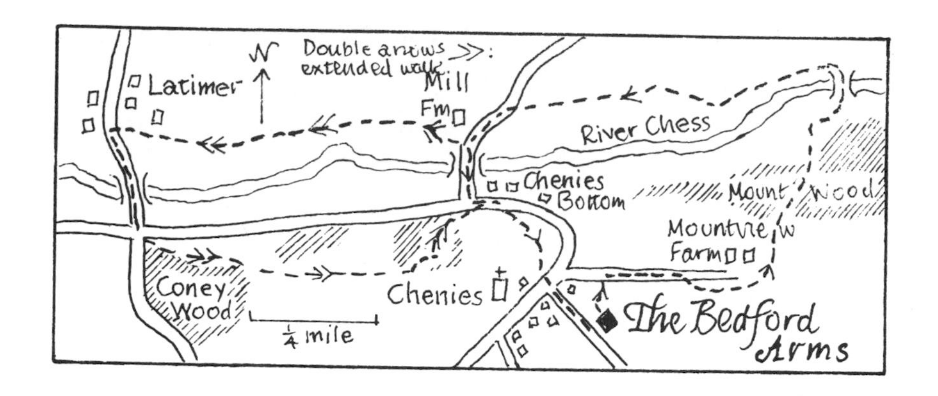

Go over the stile and turn right to follow a lane over a small footbridge across the fast-flowing little river, famous hereabouts for its watercress beds. Just past the ford take the marked footpath on the left over fields and stiles with wonderful open views along the valley, then through a little wood and on, over another stile, on to a narrow lane where you turn left towards Chenies Bottom. (The walk can be extended here – see next paragraph.) Go over a charming little curved river bridge and past Dodd's Mill on the left and follow the lane to a T-junction at a more busy road. To the left, on the other side of the road, the next path is visible a few yards ahead and up a dozen steps opposite the impressive porched entrance of Chenies Place. Follow the path through woodland above, and parallel with the road and then on to the road itself just outside the village of Chenies. Go through the gap at the end of the path and turn right on to the road to walk alongside the village green. At a T-junction on the far side turn left past delightful early 19th century red-brick cottages and timber-framed houses to return to the Bedford Arms on the left of the road.

To extend the walk here (double arrows on map) cross the road instead of turning left, to follow a bridle-track (Chess Valley Walk) through a farmyard and on over the flat fields in the valley alongside the Chess, sometimes quite deep and chuckling along and sometimes barely visible among the clumps of water weed. The track leads to a stile/gate on to a small lane where you turn left. The delightful old village of Latimer lies in the hollow just to the right. Walk up the lane to a crossroads and here, looking across the intersection, it is possible to see on the left-hand opposite corner, a stile up a grassy bank and a few rudimentary steps. Go over the stile and, bearing slightly left, walk across the field to the corner of Coney Wood and go over a stile in the fence on the far side. Here turn left to follow the path, hugging the wood edge and then across an open field to cross another stile with Greathouse Farm visible on the right. Cross the next field to go over a stile tucked into the right-hand corner and then another immediately on the left into the wood. Follow the well-defined path as it meanders gently downhill through the trees to the road. Bear left at the first fork, bear right at the second fork and left after a few yards as the path descends more steeply to the road emerging opposite the lane crossed earlier. Here turn right and walk carefully up the narrow and quite busy little road for about 200 yards to the next footpath up steps opposite the porch of Chenies Place. Follow the same route as for the shorter walk from here.

24 **Forty Green**
The Royal Standard of England

Forty Green is a tiny hamlet on the outskirts of Beaconsfield new town and lies in a fold of hills surrounded by beech woods, a peaceful and gentle little place. When the church used by William Penn (of Quaker and Pennsylvania fame) was dedicated in 1213, an inn called The Ship stood on the site of the Royal Standard of England. The hamlet was caught up in the Royalist and Roundhead skirmishes in the surrounding woodland during the Civil War and the inn became the Royalist headquarters. They renamed it The Standard and rumour has it that Charles I actually hid in the inn. It is certain that after the Restoration in 1660 Charles II gave his consent to the renaming of the inn The Royal Standard of England; perhaps the only inn with this splendid name in the country. It has an exciting collection of Civil War memorabilia: rifles, powder flasks, bugles, brass and copper articles and old needlework samplers. The walls are of magnificently preserved carved oak panelling and there are some very old stained-glass windows. Entry to the bars is via a flagged passage worn into a deep groove in the middle by the ages and ages of feet walking over it. To the left are two small rooms suitable for children, who are not permitted in the main bar which is beautifully furnished with carved oak settles and huge, deep fireplaces. The enormous car park is an indication, if such were needed, of the popularity today of this ancient inn. The garden is dominated by a huge old horse-chestnut tree in whose shade wooden tables and stools stand. Benches and tables are also plentiful at the front, behind the high front hedge and between flower-beds and gaily coloured hanging baskets.

There are a number of real ales served on hand-pump, two of which were once brewed on the premises. The recipes for Owd Roger and Royal Standard were sent on to Marston's who now supply the beer. Brakspear SB, Marston's Pedigree and a great many malt whiskies are also served, as are fruit wines. House wines, a red and two white, are served by the glass. The drinks are not cheap but the excellent food, served from a cold buffet at the far end of the bar, is extremely reasonable and generous. The inn makes a speciality of home-made pies such as rabbit, pork and bacon, pork and chestnut, beef and smoked oyster and venison pie all served with bountiful salads and a hunk of delicious crusty bread and butter. Further along the buffet are lots of cheeses and a mouth-watering selection of home-made sweets. Opening times are from 11 am to 3 pm and from 5.30 pm to 11 pm except Sundays when the inn is open from 11 am to 3 pm and from 7 pm to 10.30 pm.

Telephone: 0494 73382.

How to get there: Beaconsfield is off junction 2 of the M40. Go via the A40 into the new town and follow the signposted lane on the left off the B474 about ¾ mile from the town. The Royal Standard of England is behind a high hedge on the right almost at the top of a slight incline. Its inn sign is easy to see on the road, just opposite the entrance and by a grass triangle.

Parking: The inn has a very large car park.

Length of the walk: 4 miles. Map: OS Pathfinder 1138 High Wycombe and Amersham (GR 922918).

You can almost hear the jingle of harness and feel the press of foot soldiers as you walk across the orchard at the start of the walk. Here is a Civil War battleground and the atmosphere is evocative.

The Walk

Turn left out of the inn on to the lane and walk downhill for 150 yards to take a marked path on the right over a stile to walk through a rather run-down cherry orchard past farm buildings on the left. The path leads steeply downhill to a stile in the corner of the orchard close to

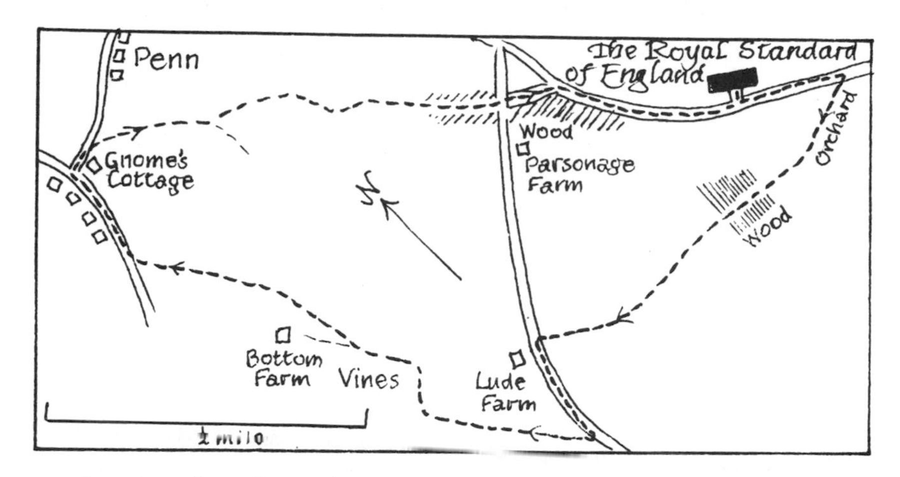

an electric pylon. Cross the stile and walk down the field, keeping the thickset hedge of hazel and bramble (very fruitful in the autumn) on the right through gently undulating scenery with views stretching away to the left. Follow the path straight ahead and then to the left into a wood along a well-defined path and over a stile to a field with a farmhouse and buildings on the right. Follow the path downhill and up again, turn right along a track towards the farm for a short distance and then go over a stile on the left and across a short field to a lane with the tall brick edifice of Lude farmhouse in front.

Turn left and walk past the farmhouse down the lane for a little over 100 yards to a path on the right which you follow, skirting the fence on the right and with a golf course ahead and to the left. Soon cross a stile on the right and turn right to walk along the field edge close to the hedge on the right. Go over a stile on the far side and follow the path alongside a large and well-managed vineyard on the left. Follow the path, then a track over fields and stiles bypassing Bottom Farm and emerging on to a lane.

Turn right to walk up the lane for about 300 yards between attractive houses set back in well-kept gardens on the outskirts of the village of Penn. After 300 yards take the marked path on the right past Gnome's Cottage and bear left at the fork following the path downhill between tall conifers and then a high laurel hedge. Go over a stile to cross the field ahead then over another where you turn right and right again on to a broad bridle-track under shady trees between stubby holly and hazel clumps with splendid views of rolling farmland glimpsed through the gaps. Because it is shady, the track can be muddy, even in summer time. At the end of the bridleway cross the lane to walk ahead down another one bearing right at the fork and finding the inn shortly on the left.

25 Chalfont St Giles
The Pheasant

The village of Chalfont St Giles is about ¼ mile from the busy A413 and this may well be why it has managed to retain its charming village atmosphere. Chalfont St Giles is probably best known for its association with the poet Milton, though he never actually owned the cottage where he lived and which is now a museum, having been purchased by public subscription in 1887 in honour of Queen Victoria's Golden Jubilee. When in 1665 the Great Plague came to London, Milton asked his friend Thomas Elwood to find him and his family a country refuge. Milton only lived in the cottage for about a year while completing his work *Paradise Lost.* The cottage now holds a great deal of memorabilia of Milton and his era.

The Pheasant lies on the A413 just to the east of the two roundabouts at the busy crossroads leading to Little Chalfont and Chalfont St Giles. The 17th century building has a pleasant creeper-covered exterior and a small patio area in the front with tables and benches and at the back via a small passage between the inn and the car park, there is a good-sized lawned garden with ample furnishing. Behind it, through an impressive brick arch, is a large children's play area with a variety of climbing toys. There are lovely views down into the Misbourne valley from the garden and barbecues are prepared there on sunny Sundays. Inside is a warm and courteous welcome from the staff behind a long bar counter. The bar has a carpeted floor and simple dark-wood furnishings; brass ornaments and pictures decorate the spaces on or between the heavy oak beams. There are two handsome stone fireplaces. A small non-smoking dining-room and a family room lead off the bar and here children are welcome. The atmosphere is quiet and comfortably friendly.

There are seven real ales on hand-pump: Benskins, Tetley Pheasant Ale (prepared especially for the inn from a secret recipe) and three or four guest ales beside another house ale, St Anton's Old Original, a mellow and smooth beer. Cider is also served on hand-pump. The huge wine list features international wines from Australia, California, Chile and every country in Europe. Five wines, two medium and one dry white and two red, are sold by the glass and half-bottles are also stocked. Meals and snacks are served every day at lunchtime and in the evenings including Sundays and a roast joint lunch is served at a give-away price on Sundays. The menu is comprehensive and includes some healthy eating salads and wholemeal baps in the summer and warming soups in winter. Specials appear on a blackboard above the fireplace and include chicken Cajun, salmon steak and vegetarian kebabs, all very reasonably priced. Six fillings may be offered in jacket potatoes, including delicious curried breast of chicken. Sandwiches, brown or white, with a variety of fillings are also prepared to order. Opening times are from 11.30 am to 3 pm and from 6 pm to 11 pm. On Sundays opening is from 12 noon to 2.30 pm and from 7 pm to 10.30 pm. It is advisable to book for a restaurant meal as the inn is very popular in the evenings.

Telephone: 0494 872113.

How to get there: From Amersham on the A413 the two roundabouts at Chalfont St Giles are approximately 3 miles from the big roundabout from the ring road outside Amersham town. Go over the mini-roundabouts and the car park for the Pheasant is on the right.

Parking: The inn has a large car park visible from the road just beyond the inn. Access is by the second opening from the road.

Length of the walk: 3½ miles. Map: OS Pathfinder 1138 High Wycombe and Amersham (GR 994938).

This gentle walk begins along the sheltered valley of the tiny river Misbourne and climbs above the village past Upper and Lower Bottom Farms to offer wide views of peaceful scenery before the descent into the village again past pleasant, well-kept houses.

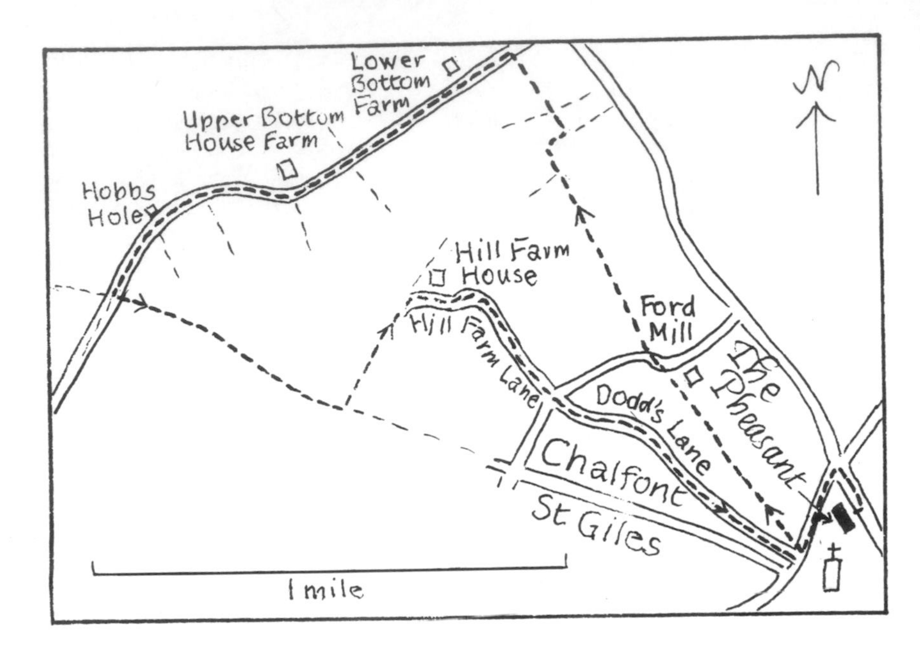

The Walk

Turn left out of the pub and left again toward the High Street of Chalfont St Giles and walk up it to take the marked path opposite the church and near the Crown public house, Stratton Chase Drive. Follow this track for a short ½ mile to a lane forming an S-bend at Ford Mill. Go across the lane to take the path immediately opposite and walk straight ahead. Ignoring all side-turnings, follow the path as it narrows between scrubby trees and then a beechwood parallel with the course of the tiny river Misbourne a field away on the right.

Go over a stile at the end of the path into a field and, keeping close to the fence on the left, follow the path across it and a little to the right at the far side to go over a stile in the hedge on the left. Cross the next small field to a stile on to a narrow lane where you turn left to walk gently uphill past the beautiful brick and timber buildings of Lower Bottom House Farm and on up to Upper Bottom House Farm, soon after which the lane curves and steepens to go past the enchanting and isolated Hobbs Hole Cottage. There are marvellous wide views of rolling, prosperous farmland all around.

After about ¼ mile, at the crest of the hill, a footpath crosses the lane so here turn left to go up three steps to a stile and follow the well-defined path ahead over fields and stiles. The last stile emerges on to a track with a handsome red-brick house on each side. Here turn right and, very shortly, arrive at a lane where you turn left on to a marked path to walk straight across a field by some splendid horse-chestnut trees to go over a stile tucked up in the left-hand corner of the hedge.

Turn left on to a path and follow it, bearing right at a T-junction, on to a gravel track and follow it past Hill Farm House, bearing leftward fairly soon past the grand 'front' entrance of the farmhouse and on downhill on the lane. At the bottom of Hill Farm Lane cross the road to Dodd's Lane opposite and follow it between pleasant houses and gardens to Botrells Lane. Here turn left and cross the road to walk down this pleasant road to the High Street again, emerging alongside the Crown. Turn left again to walk back uphill to the Pheasant and the parked car. Opposite the exit of Botrells Lane, on the far side of the village green, is a little shop with the tempting name of 'Tea-Time'.

26 Lane End
The Clayton Arms

Lane End was an early settlement of chair-makers who would have bought their chair-legs and spoke backs from 'bodgers' working in the nearby beechwoods. There are still workshops in the village but most have converted to other light industry now. Two ponds in the village centre, the Mill and the Foundry, were both used at one time in a local chair factory and Hobb's Iron Foundry.

The Clayton Arms was built by the Clayton family who retreated to Lane End in 1665 to escape the Great Plague in London; the inn is dated 1667, the year Sir Robert Clayton became Lord Mayor of London. The inn stands on the corner of a crossroads, a pleasant square whitewashed building decorated, in the summer, with numerous colourful hanging baskets. It was originally built as the manor house and the Clayton family later owned a great deal of the land around Lane End. There is the usual ghost – 'the lady in red' – but she has not put in an appearance lately. Extensive renovation, carefully and beautifully carried out in 1986, revealed an ancient fireplace and a multitude of original oak beams in the bars. The inn sign bears the arms of the Clayton family.

In front of the inn is a pleasant patio area with flowers in tubs among the tables and chairs. Inside is an enormous carpeted bar; the counter services customers on three sides of the room. It is furnished with upholstered banquettes and dark-wood tables and chairs. The walls are covered in charmingly sentimental Victorian prints and there are a vast number of copper and brass ornaments decorating ledges and beams all around. To the right of the entrance is a small snug bar with a huge squadgy sofa and settles surrounded by the same dark-wood chairs and tables. There are games machines and discreet piped music. Beyond the bar is an airy dining-room, thoughtfully and quietly furnished and with more horse brasses on the many cross-beams and uprights. Two large fireplaces ensure warmth in winter. Children are permitted in the bar area if they are eating but it is stressed that they must be well-behaved.

The real ales on hand-pump are Ruddles County Ale, Old Luxters, a local Real Barn Ale and Wadworth 6X. House wines, one red and three white, are served by the glass and there is an extensive wine list. Opposite the entrance is a series of blackboards on which the day's/week's events are listed along with the food and drink specials of the day; on my visit these included gammon steak, stuffed peppers in a Clayton 'brunch' and delicious home-made soup, bursting with vegetables, and served piping hot with generous portions of French bread. The large bar menu included filled French sticks, ploughman's lunches of cheeses or pâté, jacket potatoes with a choice of five fillings and a number of incredibly inexpensive main dishes, some of them vegetarian. Opening times are from 11 am to 11 pm from Monday to Friday. On Saturday the inn is open at 11.30 am until 3 pm and at 5.30 pm to 11 pm. On Sunday opening times are from 12 noon to 2.30 pm and from 7 pm to 10.30 pm.

Telephone: 0494 881269.

How to get there: From Marlow town take the B482 toward Stokenchurch and Lane End is approximately 5 miles from the town. The Clayton Arms lies on the right just into the village.

Parking: On the right of the pub is a reasonable sized car park which local shoppers are permitted to use when the pub is closed.

Length of the walk: 4 miles. Map: OS Pathfinder 1138 High Wycombe and Amersham (GR 808916).

The walk starts quite high up in the Chiltern village of Lane End and weaves down and uphill again, crossing and re-crossing the M40 motorway, to return over the fields behind the village houses.

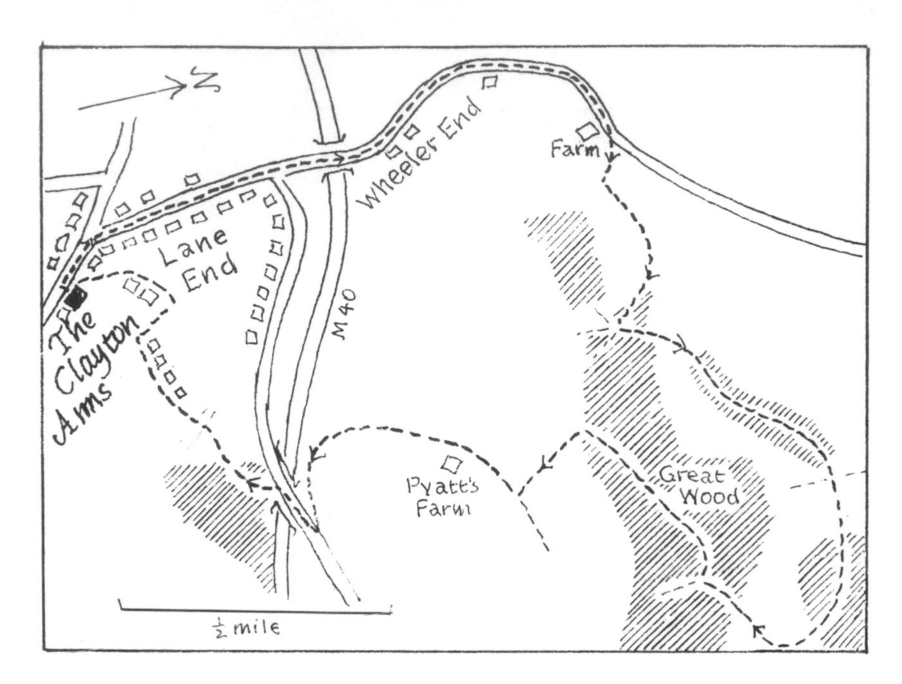

The Walk

Turn right out of the pub and right at the crossroad as for Wheeler End. The two ponds are on the right, one after the other, and have a population of large white ducks living on them. Part of the common, surrounded by pretty flint and brick cottages and houses, lies on the left. Turn left at an intersection, following the road over the M40 toward Wheeler End. There are superb open views here and magnificently colourful trees, especially in autumn dress.

Soon you reach the hamlet of Wheeler End, surrounding a village green, and with the old school building and the pub on the right. Follow the road across the common, bearing slightly right and ignoring side turnings, and then downhill alongside a delightful strip of colourful mixed woodland. Soon pretty cottages in well-kept gardens are passed on the right while, to the left, the bracken of the common seems to extend for miles. A square and uncompromising red-brick 19th century farmhouse is reached, surrounded by splendid flint barns.

Just past the farm, take the marked path on the right over a gate/stile and cross the small field diagonally to a second gate in the opposite hedge and cross by a stile against it to walk to the right downhill alongside the hedge towards Great Wood and an excuse for a stile in the extreme right corner of the field. Go on alongside the wood edge and, after 200 yards, take the stile on the left into the wood and follow the path through the lovely beechwood. At a major track junction, turn sharply right. After a few yards cross another intersection and take the narrow footpath uphill into the wood. Follow the path through this wood and over a stile on its far side to take the path across a small open field. On the far side go over a stile on to a bridle-track where you turn right to follow the track past Pyatt's Farm and on for a good mile to turn right over a bridge to cross the M40 again.

Cross the road here to enter a track marked West Wycombe Shooting Ground and immediately turn right again on to a footpath through woodland. Bear left and then right at the wood edge and go straight across a tarmacked drive to follow the well-worn path over fields, bright in summer with willow-herb and yellow ragwort, behind the gardens of houses to a stile in the far right corner. Here turn left to walk down the road and take the path after a short while on the right beside a grassy play area. Turn left at the junction to walk back into Lane End to emerge beside the patio of the Clayton Arms on the left.

27 Fingest
The Chequers

The village of Fingest lies in a deep beech-fringed dry valley in the very heart of the Chiltern countryside. The massive twin-saddleback tower of the church dominates both the tiny church itself and the huddle of flint and brick houses and cottages and the Chequers Inn. The tower of St Bartholemew's is Norman, nearly 120 metres tall and with walls over a metre thick. The present nave is joined to the tower by a 12th century arch. North of the churchyard is the site of a palace which once belonged to the Bishops of Lincoln.

The Chequers inn is opposite the church on the left-hand side of the road, a small, square red-brick 18th century building right on the roadside and adorned with colourful hanging baskets in the summer. Beyond it is a beautiful and spacious garden with an ample supply of tables and chairs under umbrellas among the flower-beds. Overlooking it all are the peaceful pastures sloping upward to the beechwood-clad hills and there are splendid views down the Hambleden valley. Inside, a warm and friendly welcome awaits the visitor. The central room of the bar has some seats built into its black-painted dado, an 18th century oak settle and a great variety of other chairs are dotted about beside small tables. The huge fireplace is decorated with antique pistols, guns and swords, jugs and mugs of pewter and brass and many decorative plates. There is a small non-smoking dining-room and a pleasantly sunny lounge with comfortable chairs and French doors on to the garden. The staff are pleasant and courteous and the service is prompt and efficient. Children are permitted in the small dining-room as well as in the garden.

This is a Brakspear house and well-kept Brakspear IPA, SB and Old Ale are all on hand-pump. House wines are sold by the glass and there is a small but interesting wine list. The Chequers is justifiably proud of its reputation for food, both bar snacks, which are incredibly reasonable, and full meals taken in the romantic little dining-room. On the menu are home-made, and very popular, spicy vegetable soup and local spicy sausages, a great variety of sandwiches and ploughman's lunches with a choice of cheeses, the latter garnished with a pretty and very generous salad. There are freshly caught trout, vegetarian dishes, roast lamb, steak and kidney pie and chicken dishes from which to make your choice. Also on offer are sumptuous and tempting puddings, mostly home-made. Opening hours are from 11 am to 3 pm and from 6 pm to 11 pm except on Sundays when the usual restrictions obtain. Food is not served on Sunday evenings.

Telephone: 0491 63335.

How to get there: From junction 4 on the M40 at High Wycombe, Fingest is 7 miles west of High Wycombe from the B482 through Lane End toward Stokenchurch. Turn left at a crossroads at Bolter End signposted Fingest 2 miles and follow the winding lane downhill to enter the village where the Chequers is on the left opposite the church.

Parking: The inn has a very commodious car park.

Length of the walk: 3½ to 4 miles. Map: OS Pathfinder 1137 Watlington and Stokenchurch (GR 779911).

This quite short walk offers a taste of the very best of the Chiltern countryside and its villages, nestling comfortably in folds of the hills. From Fingest the route forges uphill to Ibstone and then downhill quite steeply to Turville before returning, more gently, to Fingest.

The Walk

Cross the road to walk along Chequers Lane opposite, alongside the church and with Fingest Manor on the left and, just beside its entrance drive, the old railed village pound where strays were kept until retrieved by their owners. No doubt a fine accompanied the release

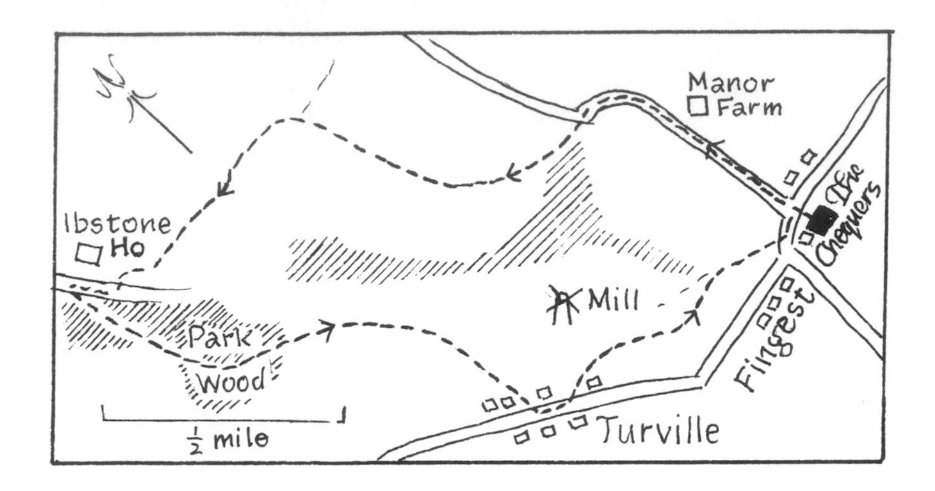

of strayed cattle, sheep or dogs. Soon Manor Farm is passed on the right; above its lovely barns and stables is a splendid blue clock-face and, nearby, a dovecote. At the sharp right bend in the road, take the marked bridleway behind metal gates on the left and follow this well-defined track through pedestrian gates into woodland and alongside fields with magnificent views of the tree-clad hills and rolling farmland below them.

Just after the third gate, take a tiny obscure path on the left into the scrubby woodland and walk ahead ignoring side turnings. Quite soon a clearing on the left is reached, looking out over parklike landscape of peaceful pastures and here there is a notice indicating the bridleway to the left and the path ahead. Turn left to walk uphill quite steeply on the bridleway, easily defined by posts on either side of the track and the white, wedding-cake-like edifice of Ibstone House high on the hill to the right. Go through a metal gate into some woods and on, steeply uphill, to a wooden gate and the lane on which the house stands. Turn right to walk the few yards up the lane past the front of Ibstone House and turn left to an obscure path exactly opposite the exit of its drive on to the lane.

Follow the path gently downhill through Park Wood, bearing right shortly on to a wide bridle-track and turning left to follow it ahead. There are wonderfully tantalising glimpses of the lovely hillsides through the trees on the right. Follow the contour of the hill along the track and through a new plantation of trees to bear right and turn left at its end, still following the track. At a sharp bend, leftward of the track, turn right to take the narrow path toward a field and a wire fence. At the fence turn left and follow the narrow little path alongside the wood edge to a stile on the right. Go over the stile and cross the field to another about halfway up the opposite hedge.

Go over this stile into an area of scrubby brush and a great variety of wild flowers. In late summer, scarlet trusses of viburnum berries vie with blackberries and rose hips to bring colour to the scene. The path falls very steeply downhill over two more stiles and across a long field to emerge on to the lane at Turville through a narrow path between houses and under a hugely leafy cherry tree.

Turn left to walk past the pretty church. A lunette in the nave has a delicate white hand and a lily by John Piper commemorating the beautification of the church in 1975 undertaken with proceeds from the sale of the Chapel of Ease at Turville Heath.

Follow the village road toward the Bull and Butcher and, against the Old School House and a red letter-box on the left, is a marked footpath which leads between houses and then across the corner of a pretty garden on the right through gates and on ahead across the field toward a stile into woodland. Above, silhouetted against the skyline, is the 18th century Copstone Mill, an unusual 12-sided smock mill featured in the film *Chitty Chitty Bang Bang*.

Go over the stile and follow the path ahead, looking downhill to the right through the beech trees to the deep valley or upward to the left where horses graze the scrubby chalkland. The path drops gently downhill to a lane over a stile. Cross this to the stile opposite and follow the path back to Fingest, turning right to go downhill where the path turns to go over the stile at the end. The Chequers is a few yards down the lane on the right.

28 Marlow
The Hare and Hounds

Bruce Watkin, in his Buckinghamshire Guide, calls Marlow the happiest town in the county. Set in an amphitheatre of chalk hills running down to a wide reach of the river Thames, the town is famous for its magnificent suspension bridge with a span of 225 ft and two towers set above the roaring weir. All Saints church can be seen behind the bridge, and the High Street, running up from it, has a delightful mix of 18th, 19th and 20th century architecture.

The Hare and Hounds lies about a mile from the town centre on the road to Henley. The low creeper-covered building, dated 1642, has a colourful array of small flower-beds and hanging baskets outside its front door and window boxes under the small low-placed windows. To the left of the inn is a quite beautiful garden of rockeries and flower-beds approached by crazy-paved paths in ups and downs and a number of wooden benches and tables where the excellent food and drink can be enjoyed along with the garden. Immediately upon entering the long low-timbered bar there is a warm welcome from the attentive staff, a table is found if it is required and the menu, on huge blackboards, is lifted down from its hooks on the beamed ceiling and is brought for inspection. A couple of steps up from the main bar is a quieter room, laid for meals and used as a dining-room in the evenings. The bar is flagged but on both sides of it the floor is carpeted and set with comfortably upholstered chairs in a muted shade of fabric; the tables are a mix of assorted shapes and sizes: all are highly polished. There is a small fruit machine and the piped music is not obtrusive. Attractive pictures of riverside scenes adorn the walls and the recesses of the three fireplaces are decorated with copper pans and dishes. The wine list, of interesting but not cheap wines, is featured as a decoration on large green bottles on the tables. The wines are available by the glass, flagon or bottle. Children are welcome anywhere as long as they are well-behaved. Beers on hand-pump are the ever-popular Boddingtons Best, Brakspear and IPA Rebellion from the Marlow brewery. Specials on the blackboard include seafood lasagne. Most especially to be recommended is a dish of smoked chicken and bacon pieces on croûtons on a bed of crisp salad and served with crusty brown bread and butter. There are baguettes with a variety of six fillings, ploughman's platter, meatballs in spicy sauce, seafood Mornay and tortellini all served with generous portions of crisp fresh salad. Opening hours are from 11 am to 3 pm and from 5.30 pm to 11 pm every day except Sunday when they are from 12 noon to 3 pm and from 7 pm to 10.30 pm.

Telephone: 0628 483343.

How to get there: The Hare and Hounds lies on the right hand side of the A4155 Marlow to Henley road, just about a mile from the town centre of Marlow.

Parking: Beside the inn is a huge car park hewn out of the chalky hillside and there is additional parking behind it.

Length of the walk: 4 miles. Map: OS Pathfinder 1157 Maidenhead and Marlow (GR 839858).

The river Thames seems tantalisingly near sometimes during this walk but it is concentrated on the wooded hillsides above the river valley.

The Walk

Cross the road to a tiny lane opposite which states that there is no vehicular access to the river and follow the lane downhill toward Low Grounds Farm. The lane is hedged and filled with scent and colour from dog-roses and bramble flowers in summer; a huge mallow is covered in sharply pink flowers later on. Soon the lane flattens out beside lush water meadows on the left and a peaceful, parklike landscape rising gently on the right. Wild flowers abound in the

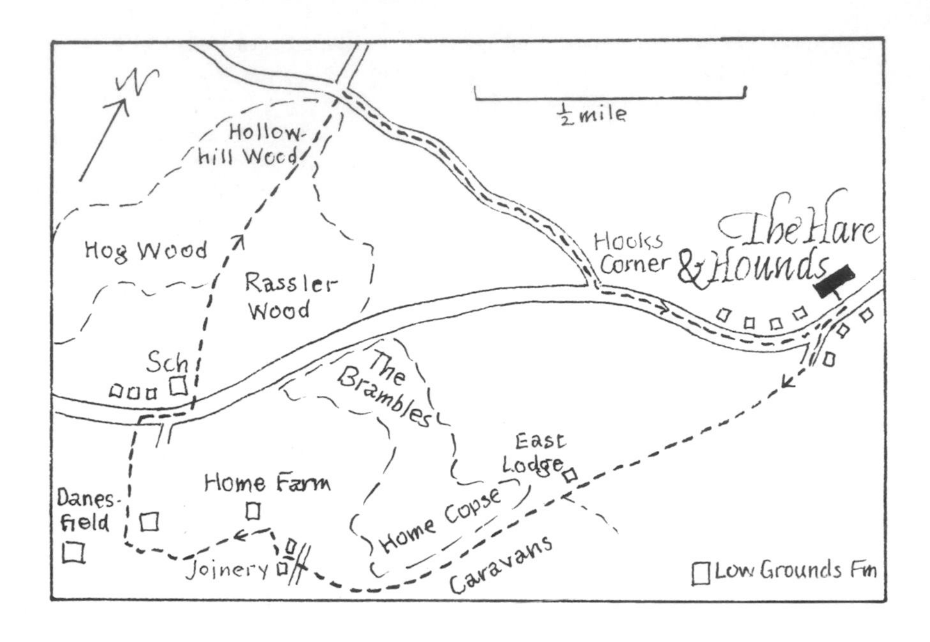

hedge-bottom and the chalk-loving butterflies hurry among them. After about ⅓ mile go straight ahead past East Lodge, keeping the large caravan park of Harleyford Marina on the left across the field. Home Copse lies on the right and, below it, tall willow-herb and huge prickly teazles grow. Go through a kissing-gate on the far side of the field to follow a little path between a fence and the woodland.

Cross a private road to rejoin the path on the far side between the buildings of Harleyford Joinery. The path is defined by large conical white-painted stones and then goes steeply uphill by some steps. Go straight ahead over a stile past Home Farm buildings and cottages and through the white wooden gate on the far side of the cottages. Follow the path round the field and then through another white gate on to a broad grass track just past the entrance to Home Farmhouse and follow the track alongside a high coniferous hedge. At the end of the hedge, under a huge chestnut tree, turn left and follow the path downhill for a few yards. At a path junction, take the path ahead and slightly right to cross the drive of Danesfield. Take the path opposite through a kissing-gate and follow it diagonally across a large field with farm buildings on the left to an exit on to the busy A4155. Turn right to walk along the road for only 200 yards or so, past the entrance to Danesfield on the right and then go across the road to take the marked path alongside the entrance to Danesfield School on the left. Follow the well-defined footpath, bearing right at a fork and keeping an eye on the white arrows painted on trees, through Hollowhill Wood.

The path emerges on to a crossroads of narrow lanes and here turn right to follow Hooks Lane, signposted for Marlow 1 ½ miles away; the Hare and Hounds is considerably closer than that! Follow the pleasantly quiet and tree-shaded lane with occasional wide views of rich farmland bordered by dark strips of woodland through the gaps in the thick hazel hedge. At Hook's Corner, overlooking meadows sweeping down to and up from the river toward Temple, turn left to walk again along the busy A4155 for about ¼ mile to the Hare and Hounds and the parked car.

29 Hambleden
The Stag and Huntsman

The peaceful and attractive little village of Hambleden lies a mile off the A4155, Marlow/Henley road; it is 3 miles from Henley and 5 miles from Marlow. The Hamble brook runs through the village to join the Thames at Mill End, on the main road. The 11th century church of St Mary dominates the village centre; its tower is decorated with four small turrets, each one bearing a weather-vane.

The Stag and Huntsman, originally called the Dog and Badger, was built in the mid 17th century but its front has been modernised, though the inside of the inn is obviously very old with narrow passages and nooks and darkened wood-panelling round the walls of the bars which are pleasantly furnished and light. There is a large grassy garden behind the inn set with benches and tables; children are permitted in the garden but not in the bars. The landlord and his team of helpers are friendly and cheerful and service is quick and efficient though the bars get very full indeed at weekend lunchtimes, despite the fact that the menu of bar snacks is kept deliberately low and restricted at that time. On Friday and Saturday evenings the small restaurant is opened for dinner where Huntsman steak features large on the menu. This is a large beef steak, smeared with dark brown sugar and grilled to caramelise the sugar and it is mouth-wateringly delicious. Chargrilled steaks, fresh salmon and many other dishes are offered. The menu is presented on a large blackboard and on weekdays includes jacket potatoes with a variety of fillings, home-made steak and kidney pie, quiche and salad, home-made soup with crusty bread and ploughman's lunches with an assortment of cheeses. Also served with 'proper' toast is a delicious home-made smoked fish pâté decorated with 'poor man's caviare' – lump-fish roe – and salad. None of the meals is expensive and most are very reasonably priced indeed.

A mile up the road is the Chiltern Valley Winery and the landlord stocks a good selection of excellent wines from there and also a real ale brewed at the winery, Old Luxters Barn Ale, which is very good. Other beers served are Brakspear Ordinary and Special, Wadworth 6X and Farmer's Glory. Four French wines are sold by the glass. Opening hours are from 11 am to 2.30 pm and from 6 pm to 11 pm on all days but Sunday when the hours are 12 noon to 2.30 pm and 7 pm to 10.30 pm.

Telephone: 0491 571227.

How to get there: The village can be approached from either Henley or Marlow on the A4155. It is signposted off the road close to Mill End. On entering the village, turn right past the front of the church and go straight ahead on the more minor of the two roads between small flint cottages and the famous emporium of H. Wheeler, butcher, who supplies the gentry for miles around with meat and game. The pub is on the left after the car park.

Parking: There is a small free car park on the right just past the Stag and Huntsman and it is safest to use this as the lane is very narrow.

Length of the walk: 3½ miles. Map: OS Pathfinder 1156 Henley-on-Thames and Wallingford (GR 783865).

Out of the quiet beauty of the little village of Hambleden, the walk climbs to quite a rugged hillside, much punished in the recent gales, and then meanders downhill and back along a lane to the village again.

The Walk

Turn right out of the pub and follow the lane past the car park and the entrance to Kenricks to walk quite steeply uphill into a small mixed woodland. There are glimpses on the left of the gently falling chalk valley whose sides are edged with beech woods. Where one of the large trees has been felled by the gales, there is a magnificent view

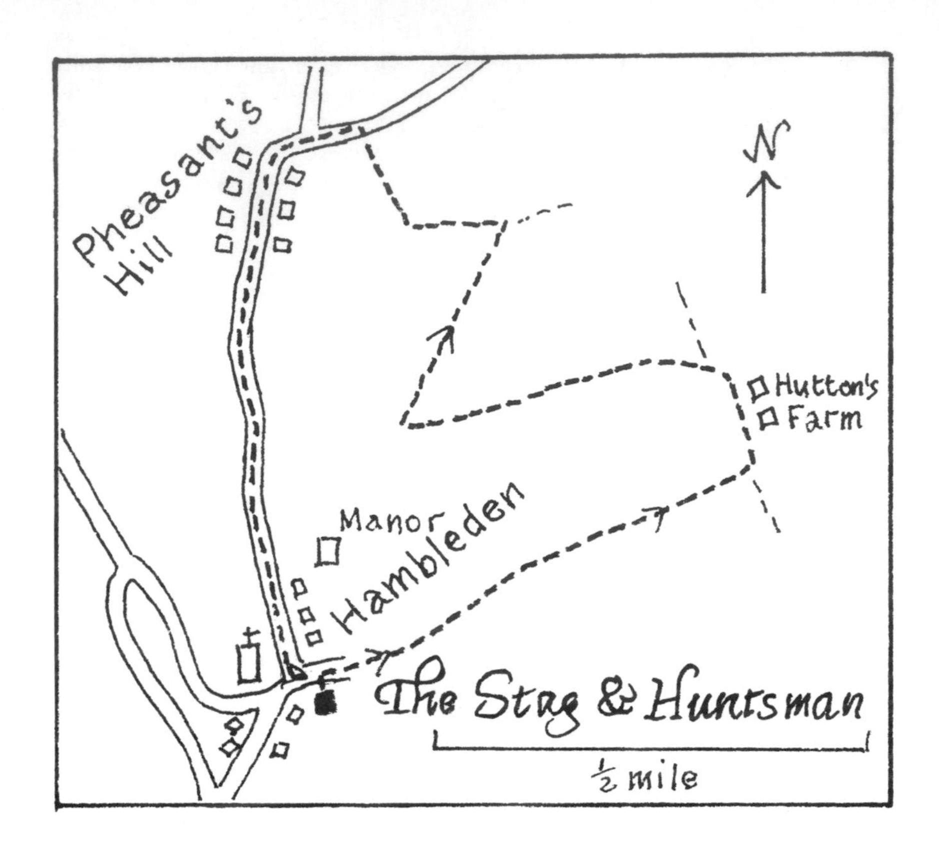

of the whole Hambleden valley. Pheasants potter in and out, rooting among the leaves at the wood edge and shortly there is evidence of a now disused chalk-pit. Follow the broad track out into open country where the flint and brick farmhouse of Hutton's Farm comes into view ahead. Just before the farmhouse, turn left into a metalled track and walk to a green metal gate. Here are magnificent airy views all around.

Go over the stile beside the gate on to a grassy track and follow it to another stile. Cross this and turn left for a few yards and then, at a junction, turn right along a well-defined path hugging the contour of the hillside. Take the left fork at the path junction and walk gently downhill toward the little settlement of Pheasant's Hill in the valley. The path narrows here and twists about to avoid fallen tree trunks. There is new plantation on each side and, among the new trees, the huge upended dish-like tree-roots have been left to provide a useful habitat for insects and for new growth. Notice how many of them have young holly bushes growing out of them. The bushes of self-sown buddleia are a lovely sight in the summer, their purple rods of flowers covered with butterflies of many varieties. The path goes gently downhill to a stile. Do not cross this but turn left to follow the narrow path to a much grander one which you cross and then turn right to follow a path through softly curving fields toward the warm red-brick and flint cottages of Pheasant's Hill.

Go through the kissing-gate at the end of the path and turn left on to a lane which you follow round past the chapel and some pleasant Victorian houses on the left. Snug little flint cottages line the road then, opposite the church is Hambleden Manor, the home of W.H. Smith, the first Viscount Hambleden and the birthplace of Lord Cardigan of the Charge of the Light Brigade fame. Turn left near the church to return to the car park.

30 Fulmer
The Black Horse

Fulmer is a well-kept little village in a deep wooded valley with tidy warm brick houses of 18th and 19th century origin in its centre and a spread of large houses in parks, surrounded by farms, studs and small paddocks for ponies. The present church of St James is a complete rebuilding of the original medieval church carried out in 1610 for the then Lord of the Manor, Sir Marmaduke Dayrell, Treasurer to the King. It has a stout studded wooden door, white with age, and a squat bell-tower. Much Victorianising restoration was done in the late 1880s and overly ornate stained-glass windows now render the interior somewhat gloomy. The outside is friendlier than the inside, to look at, at least.

The Black Horse is the only pub in the village and was built as a hut for building materials during the building of the church next door and then used for petty sessions as early as 1681. The present building dates from 1720 and additions have been made at various times later. It is a simple, unsophisticated pub without pretentions to any sort of grandeur but it has a wonderfully cosy and friendly atmosphere; it is obviously the meeting-place for all the local people who crowd the small, wooden-floored middle bar furnished with long cushioned settles behind plain wooden tables, the walls decorated with attractive pen drawings of the pub and the church beyond. The lounge bar is plainly carpeted and furnished with settles and stools around square tables. On the walls are photos of the local morris dancers performing on Fulmer Day, an event which takes place in June each year. There is a games machine in this bar. The Fulmer bar is carpeted and quiet, furnished with the same cushioned settles and tables. The two end bars have fine old fireplaces and one bar counter serves all three bars. Service is friendly and efficient. On hand-pump are Courage Directors and Courage Best. House wines, a red and two white, are served by the glass. The menu is small and interesting, the food home-made and good and the prices extremely low. On the menu there is always a home-made soup served with a big crusty roll, jacket potatoes are served with a variety of fillings including a lavish chicken curry, deep-fried mushrooms or sausage and cheese. Ploughman's lunches with a choice of cheeses, and sandwiches, including doorsteps and smoked salmon with cream cheese, are prepared to order and very reasonably priced. Outside is a large, lawned garden with a big children's play area beyond. There are also tables and benches at the front of the pub. Well-behaved children are welcome in the quieter bars and the garden. Opening hours are 11 am to 3 pm and 6 pm to 11 pm Monday to Saturday and on Sunday 12 noon to 3 pm and 7.30 pm to 10.30 pm.

Telephone: 0753 663183.

How to get there: From Gerrards Cross on the A40, go through traffic lights at the crossroads and take the next major turn signposted Fulmer into an unclassified road. Follow the road over the M40 and downhill into Fulmer village; the Black Horse lies on the left just past the church which is on a bend.

Parking: The pub has a large car park.

Length of the walk: 3½ to 4 miles. Maps: OS Pathfinder 1157 Maidenhead and Marlow and 1158 Hillingdon and Wembley (GR 998856).

The south of the county can bring very different views from either the very steep Chiltern slopes or the gentler undulations of the north. The landscape is more heathlike and the farmland enclosed, prosperous and lush.

The Walk

Turn right out of the pub to walk past the church to take the marked path immediately past it on the right. Follow the path over a stile and

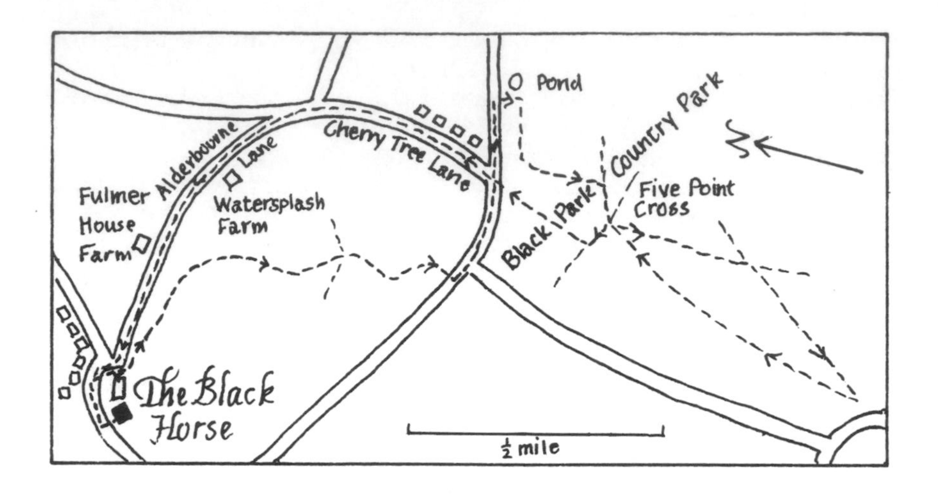

across the field ahead to another one in the hedge opposite and cross the next field diagonally to a small gate in the right-hand corner. Go through the gate and, in the next field, walk steadily uphill, with marvellous views all round, to go very slightly left toward another small gate buried in the opposite hedge. This leads on to a narrow path between vigorously growing rhododendron bushes which are a colourful delight in the springtime. The path leads across the drive of a rather splendid house and then, on the far side of the drive, the narrow path continues, to emerge, finally, on to the main drive of this estate of grand houses. Here turn right and follow the drive down to the main road.

At the road turn left and follow the wooded way for about ½ mile, round a sharp left-hand bend and past the exit of Cherry Tree Lane on to the road. Almost immediately after this enter Black Park Country Park, a large area of managed woodland, wetland and heath in the care of Buckinghamshire County Council. Walk ahead from the entrance and, after a few yards, bear left to follow a broad drive, past a pond on the left, to Five Point Cross. Here bear slightly right on to another broad drive and, crossing an intersection, turn right again at another intersection through open scrubland and areas of deep shady mixed woodland. Walk ahead to another main intersection opposite a plantation of new oak trees leading shortly to the Five Point Cross again.

Now turn left, leaving a wooden bench and the original track on the right-hand side and, after about ¼ mile, turn right at a T-junction on to a broad gravel path. Follow this ahead and then bear round to meet the original path quite close to the entrance from the road. Turn left to reach the entrance, left on to the road and almost immediately right into Cherry Tree Lane.

Walk down this pretty lane with well-kept houses and gardens on the right, turning left at the T-junction at the foot of the hill with a ford across the road ahead. Just before reaching the ford turn left again into Alderbourne Lane and follow it past Watersplash Farm on the left where hefty, hugely caped Charolais beef cattle graze. High on the hill to the right is the lovely red-brick Regency Fulmer House standing in its peaceful park-like grounds and, close to the road, the busy and prosperous-looking Fulmer House Farm. Further on are some more pretty 19th and 20th century houses and cottages. At the T-junction turn left to walk back past the church to the Black Horse again.